New Jersey History

PETER KROSS

The Middle Atlantic Press
Wilmington, Delaware 19899

This book is dedicated to the memory of my father, Milton Kross, who would have wanted to tell the world of its publication.

Special thanks to Jim Emolo, the editor of *Dateline Journal*. Some of the stories in this book have appeared in this publication.

NEW JERSEY HISTORY

A MIDDLE ATLANTIC PRESS BOOK

Copyright © 1987 by Peter Kross

First Middle Atlantic Press printing, August 1987

ISBN: 0-912608-45-5

Library of Congress Cataloging-in-Publication Data

Kross, Peter, 1948–
  New Jersey history.

  Bibliography: p.
  Includes index.
  1. New Jersey—History.   I. Title.
F134.K74   1987   974.9   87-11171
ISBN 0-912608-45-5

The Middle Atlantic Press, Inc.
848 Church Street
Wilmington, Delaware 19899

Manufactured in the United States of America

CONTENTS

Introduction

Over the years I've listened as New Jersey has taken the brunt of more than a few good natured jokes. It is not uncommon to hear people say that they went through New Jersey on the way to someplace else. Many people visualize the entire state as the stretch of the turnpike that goes through a large area of industry and refineries.

But is that what New Jersey is all about? Or is there another, far different New Jersey, one that most people often forget or have little knowledge of?

In the winter, thousands of people flock to our rugged mountains for skiing and cross country walks amid some of the most beautiful scenery in the Northeast. Summer time beckons families to sparkling lakes and miles of pristine, white shore that runs from the tip of Long Beach Island down to Cape May.

While the present use of these lands brings much pleasure, their past echoes with the adventures of the individuals that shaped the young New Jersey. In reality, from the early explorers to the dawn of the 20th century, the story of New Jersey is an account of America itself.

From New Jersey the lives of presidents, kings, adventurers, spies, seamen, traitors, patriots, builders, dreamers and warriors have come forth.

The echoes of the Great Falls of Passaic, whose thunderous waters still sound next to the sledgehammers of urban renewal, of pirates, whose buried treasure may still be under the sands of the Jersey shore, of traitors like Aaron Burr, who, from our banks, planned to make his own country in the west can be heard in New Jersey History today. It is the story of the mysterious Pine Barrens, now preserved for generations to come. Of soldiers like Phil Kearney, Judson Kilpatrick and Captain Sawyer, whose fate caused an international incident.

It is also the story of the beginnings of people such as Stephen Crane, whose poetry still haunts us today. And of the Roeblings, who worked for years to build the Brooklyn Bridge.

The initial reactions to stories that have appeared in earlier publications has provided me with satisfaction at being able to bring the story of the people, "to the people." Readers frequently respond, "I didn't know that happened in New Jersey."

It is my hope that this book will bring the story of New Jersey home to all those interested in the richness of the past and the people who have dared to shape its destiny.

Early Man in New Jersey

OUR EARLIEST ANCESTORS settled in what is now New Jersey, thousands of years before recorded history. There are numerous theories as to how prehistoric man made his way to the American continent. One theory suggests that he simply "walked" here, during the ice age, via the Bering Strait, where it is believed that a huge land bridge, which connected Asia to Alaska, once existed. Another theory holds that centuries before Columbus discovered America, Norwegian adventurers had already set foot on the New World.

Many bits of tantalizing evidence, found during the course of the eighteen hundreds, suggests that a large ancient culture once lived in New Jersey's backyards. In 1872, searchers located the long sought "Lenape Stone," in the Delaware Valley. The stone indicated that the Lenape Indians, the first tribe to inhabit the area, had coexisted with a race of people that have since become extinct.

In various other parts of New Jersey, searchers have used methods such as carbon dating on tools found in dig sites. Objects made of both flint and argillite have been found. Such tests provide strong evidence that an older race of people, prior to the Lenape Indians, resided in New Jersey.

The banks of the Delaware River have provided a rich source of clues to prehistoric man. The remains of an ancient culture were found near Warfords Rock, outside Frenchtown, N.J., buried 2½ feet below ground level. They are believed to have been found in their original position and location.

Two miles south of Trenton, the Abbot Farm can be found on the banks of the Delaware. It is the largest aboriginal village site found in the state, stretching for 3½ miles along the river. Beginning in 1872, Dr. Abbott began unearthing artifacts for study. By 1882, he concluded that many of the items found belonged to a race that lived in the early glacial age. These people were called Palaeolithic Man. Based on his findings, he also concluded that an unknown intermediate race, after Palaeolithic man, and before the Lenapes, had also existed.

Finally, in our own time, an exciting discovery was made in the Passaic Valley town of Chatham. Here the remains of a prehistoric Mastodon were found standing erect.

Regardless of the theory one chooses to believe as to how man first arrived in New Jersey, there remains a host of artifacts to be discovered and pages of unwritten history to be chronicled on early man.

New Jersey's Early Explorers

DURING THE AGE of discovery many early adventurers from Europe sailed to what is now the United States, in search of new lands to conquer.

In the late 1400's and early 1500's, explorers such as Henry Hudson, Esteban Gomez and Giovanni da Verrazzano sailed along the North American coast from New Foundland to Florida looking for new territory.

Many of these men passed by what is now New Jersey, en route to other, more distant places.

But who were the brave adventurers who laid claim to the land that is our state today? Where did they come from and what mark did they leave behind?

One of the first travelers to locate land in our region was a Dutch skipper called Adriaen Block who, in 1612, sailed into the Hudson River. Block skippered a convoy from Holland but when he started to explore the Hudson his lead ship was destroyed by hostile Indians. Block took his survivors to their backup vessel, the *Restless,* and began an exploration that would take him around Long Island Sound, Narragansett Bay and Cape Cod. Coming further south Block erected a fort near present-day Jersey City as a guard post and named it Block House.

The man first credited with the actual "discovery" of New Jersey was a sea captain from Holland, Cornelius Mey.

Mey was the first Director General of the New Netherlands Company and in 1623 he started to explore the Hudson River and the South River, now called Delaware Bay.

Unlike his predecessor, Adriaen Block, Mey found the Indians less troublesome and, like Block, he named a strip of land he discovered after himself, "Cape May."

With the Dutch now entrenched in the New World, Mey set up a town near the present city of Gloucester. He named the stronghold Fort Nassau, which became the first permanent settlement in New Jersey. Mey traded peacefully with the local Indians who saw the new white settlers as both adversaries and potential new markets. Mey developed a good relationship with the Indians and, in a letter he sent to the Dutch East India Company in Holland that bankrolled his expedition, he wrote that it was his policy to treat the Indians as equals in order to keep the peace.

Three years after Mey's discovery of new territories the East India Company ordered him home and he was replaced by another adventurer named Peter Minuit. Minuit later explored areas of present-day New York.

If Mey is credited with being the first discoverer of New Jersey, the honor of first land pioneer goes to David Petersen De Vries, also a Dutchman.

Following in Mey's footsteps, DeVries established a series

of trading posts in New Jersey and by 1630, he'd built the first land colony called South River.

De Vries brought with him two boats, cattle, supplies and tools to build a town.

At the South River location De Vries and his men planted grain and tobacco but their best source of income came from whaling.

At the helm of his sloop, the *Walrus,* De Vries and his crew would ply the waters catching as many whales as they could and would use the meat as food and fuel for the colony.

De Vries returned to Holland and two years later made another expedition to America. Upon his return he found that the remaining settlers had all been killed in Indian raids.

Soon other explorers came to New Jersey to fashion a series of outposts along the shore.

One of the first to arrive was an English sea captain, Lieutenant Robert Evelyn. Lt. Evelyn was the first white man to penetrate the rugged country behind the coast line of New Jersey.

Men like Mey, Block and De Vries were the forerunners of the settlers who would discover a new continent and write a fresh chapter in our history.

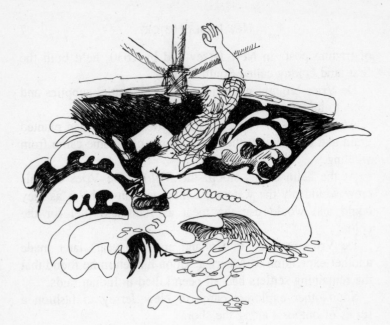

The River Man–Jonas Cattel

THERE ARE MANY stories of men who made their homes along the rivers and in the wilds of early New Jersey. They were generally rugged individuals, able to survive away from the mainstream of civilization. While their stories and exploits have been handed down from generation to generation, it would seem that many of the events of their lives have grown in stature so that it becomes impossible to distinguish truth from fiction.

One such famed individual is Jonas Cattel, born in Woodbury in 1758. He appears to have lived quite an exciting life, being both a hunter and a soldier.

During the American Revolution, Cattel worked as a soldier of fortune on the American side. During the many battles against the British, who occupied New Jersey, Jonas captured a number of troops. Many belonged to Count Donap's allied German Hessians located near Red Bank.

Following the war, Jonas returned to his home in South Jersey, back to what he considered the important activities in life: fishing and hunting. For a while he worked for the Gloucester Country Fox Hunting Club.

But the story that made Jonas famous was his encounter with a great sturgeon. Jonas caught the huge fish while casting in his boat. The great fish took both Jonas and his boat upstream, against the fast current. But luckily, Jonas managed to free himself from the sturgeon's grasp.

The incident is said to have had a second chapter for Jonas. Once again out in his boat, he caught the same fish a second time. The mighty fish pulled poor Jonas upstream at an even faster clip than before. But this time danger lay in their way.

The fish dragged Jonas right into a covered bridge where cattle were being taken to the other side. The fish plowed into the bridge, causing the cattle to fall into the river. While the fish lunched on several of the helpless cattle, Jonas safely escaped once more.

Shortly thereafter, many ranchers in the Valley noticed that some of their cattle began to vanish without a trace.

The worried herders set out to investigate and they reported seeing a large fish eating their missing cattle.

Looking for a scapegoat, they blamed Jonas, the man who "rode" the fish. There was talk that Jonas was a friend of the fish and that he should be held responsible for the damage the animal had done.

Jonas, being the fair man he was, spent a great deal of money repaying the cattlemen for their loses.

In his later years, Jonas still could walk 120 miles from dawn to dusk and he died at 91, one of the most famous men in South Jersey.

Pirates on the Delaware Bay

THE SEA HAS always played an important role in the history of New Jersey, beginning with the first explorers who came to our shores in search of new lands and treasure.

The history of the South Jersey coast, especially the area along the Delaware Bay, witnessed more than its share of adventurers, who plied its rocky shores seeking the gold that lay in their path. It was in the 1600's that men, whom we today call pirates, roamed the crystal clear waters off Delaware Bay, in search of fortunes.

One pirate haven in New Jersey was a small town called Stons Creek. It was to this remote place that pirates would come and anchor their ships, mend their sails and hide from the law. One of their favorite gathering places was Bricks Mill & Tavern at Jericho.

Below the banks of Stons Creek was Woods Landing. There pirates used an inland road which led from the creek to Bicky Mill, five miles away. They then transported goods from one ship to another. This road was nicknamed "The Devil's Highway."

One famous pirate to roam the waters of South Jersey was Edward Teach, also known as Blackbeard. He had a long flowing black beard, he dressed in silk and velvet, always with a brace of pistols in his belt. He is said to have been the most cunning of all pirates who raided the ships of the Atlantic coast.

Blackbeard operated near the seaboard towns of the Black Neck region of the Delaware bay. During the winter months he and his crew lived on land in a log cabin. Over the centuries, people have claimed to have heard strange noises coming from the remains of Blackbeard's house.

Another notorious pirate who sailed into the Delaware Bay was Captain William Kidd. He was born in Dundee, Scotland, the son of a Puritan minister. In 1769 he was approached by Lord Belmont, Governor of New England, who asked him to lead an expedition to capture pirates who were raiding British ships in the Caribbean.

Kidd roamed the seas, capturing ships. Belmont turned on Kidd when the Captain was perceived as too lenient towards the ships he captured. Lord Belmont then declared Captain Kidd a pirate. Captain Kidd reportedly settled in the small islands and marches of Bacons Neck, and then in Tindalls and Nancy Island, where he was rumored to have buried large amounts of treasure.

An article in a Philadelphia newspaper, dated July 1, 1766, reads, ". . . there arrived in this government in a ship directly from Malligasco. They are part of Kidd's gang. About 20 of them landed in this place. (Lower Delaware Bay) About 16 more landed at Cape May in West Jersey. She is a very rich ship—all her loading in rich East India Baile Goods to a very great value, besides an abundance of money.''

On May 23, 1801, Captain Kidd went to the gallows. On August 8, 1870, two men returning up Salem Creek found a large wooden box sticking out of the sand. They returned that night, and during a violent thunder storm, pried open the wooden box. Inside they found a treasure trove of silver plate and coins. Could this have been part of Captain Kidd's treasure?

Today the rattling chains of pirates are gone, along with the Jolly Roger that flew from the wooden masts of their schooners. But the lure and the wealth of legends they left behind still remain.

The Legend of Tom Quick

ANYONE INTERESTED IN the folklore of the old West knows the names of the famous gunfighters that roamed the cattle towns of the old West dispensing their own type of justice. The best known names are Billy the Kid and Wyatt Earp.

But there was a man in the Delaware Valley in the late 1700's whose quest for vengeance took him on a life-long journey to find the killers of his father.

Tom Quick Jr. lived with his family in Milford, Pennsylvania in the late 1700's. He was born in upstate New York on December 22, 1713 and throughout his early life wandered with his kin between New Jersey and Pennsylvania. In later life young Tom married Margriete Dekker and they had ten children.

Tom Jr. was a normal child who liked to hunt in the wooded forests and fish in the crystal clear streams of the Delaware Valley.

But one dark night in 1756, while Tom was out in the woods with his father, an event so shocking took place that Tom would devote the rest of his life to coming to terms with it.

On that fateful night Tom Quick Sr., his son Tom Jr. and a son-in-law were traveling through the wooded Delaware River Valley when they were attacked by a band of Indians.

The Indian raiding party moved swiftly and when the incident was over Tom Quick Sr. lay dead.

Tom and his brother-in-law fired back at the Indians as the assailants fled deeper into the forest.

With his father dead, Tom and his party fanned out to search for those responsible for the heinous crime. They found the body of a dead Indian they'd killed and followed fresh tracks through the woods.

They soon encountered a party of 15 Lenni-Lenape Indians camped in clearing not far from where Tom's father had been murdered.

The white men swooped down into the camp of the sleeping Indians and killed six before the final shot was fired.

As the days and months passed young Tom discovered that none of the braves they'd killed in the raid had been responsible for his father's death. What followed was Tom's bloody fulfillment, to seek the slayer of his father no matter how long it took.

As the years went by Tom became known as Tom Quick–Indian Slayer, who carried a powerful rifle nicknamed Long Tom.

As Tom's legend grew and the years since that awful night flew by, an Indian known as Muswink began to brag that he killed Tom Quick Sr. He also said that he'd kill young Tom if he got the chance.

At this point in the story the facts become difficult to determine because there are various accounts of what happened next.

Some people who lived in the Delaware Valley said that Tom Jr. hunted Muswink for 40 years while others said it was much less.

It is believed that one night Tom Jr. met Muswink at a tavern kept by a man called Decker on the Neversink River near Port Jervis, New York.

Eyewitnesses who were in the bar said that Muswink bragged that he'd killed Tom Quick Sr. and he is supposed to have told the crowd that he no longer sought out young Tom, that the hatred of so many years had been buried.

After hearing Muswink's remarks and not believing them, Tom is supposed to have pulled a gun on the Indian and then taken him out of the tavern.

James Quinlain's account of the events that followed differ.

Tom took Muswink on the road going from Wurtsboro to Carpenters Point. Tom stopped a carriage containing Muswink and shot him, taking back his father's buckles, cufflinks and buttons that Muswink wore. After the killing, Tom returned to the tavern and told his friends what happened.

A short time later Tom Jr. was arrested at Carpenters Point, near Port Jervis. He was held at Decker's Tavern but was rescued from his confinement by his friends.

Tom fled to Pennsylvania to the home of Cornelius De Witt.

As the years passed, public excitement concerning Tom's exploits ended along with the police hunt.

No one really knows what happened to Tom Quick. He is supposed to have fled to Canada. Tom died on December 20, 1795 and in Milford, Pennsylvania there is a statue in honor of the Delaware Valley's most famous outlaw.

Mystery In The Pine Barrens

TODAY AS WE drive south on the Garden State Parkway en route to the shore with its sparkling white beaches, the traveler passes through one of the most historic and hidden areas of New Jersey, the desolate Pine Barrens.

This huge and heavily forested area of the state covers 1,875 square miles and is located halfway between Boston and Richmond.

Not many people live in the Pine Barrens today, the old iron mills have long since failed and the once prosperous towns are only a memory.

But it wasn't always like that. The Barrens were the home

of a great number of people and many events in the history of the state took place there.

Because of its isolation the Pine Barrens became a haven for people who, for their own reasons, wanted to escape the problems of the day. Among the many who found refuge in the Barrens were Tories, people in favor of the British during the Revolutionary War, Quakers who wanted to preserve their own religious identity, British deserters and many negro slaves including a black doctor, James Still, also called "Black Jim."

Descendents of the first Indian tribes in New Jersey settled in the Barrens and following a massacre of Indians in West Jersey, they were given 3,258 acres in the desolate woods. The area was called Bortherton and it was the first Indian reservation in North America.

If the Pine Barrens were a natural place for the respectable seeking their own way of life, they were also the home of the less scrupulous.

Smugglers by the hundreds descended on the natural camouflage to start their own illegal businesses. The smugglers used the many inlets that ran from the Atlantic through the Barrens to sell such items as coffee, tea, molasses and sugar, and clandestinely send them to the nearby ports of New York and Philadelphia. Their precious cargo would be transferred to wagons and shipped over the dirt backroads where it would be loaded on to ships or other means of transportation.

One of the most famous of the Pine Barrens smugglers was John Mathis, who shipped lumber to the islands of the Caribbean and imported rum.

But the most important industry was iron.

A natural phenomenon of the Barrens was the cause of their success in iron production. When rain water fell on the fallen pine needles, the litter became sufficiently acidic to eat out iron from the sand. The molten iron moved to underground streams and oxidized on contact with air, thus forming a patch on the surface.

Many boom towns sprang up in the Barrens rivaling the gold rush towns of California in later years.

Skilled iron makers made thousands of cannonballs that were sent to Washington's army at Valley Forge. Cannons, as well as shot, were available to the Americans from the arms made in the Barrens and were used in the War of 1812. Among the many heroes who benefited from the arms made in the Barrens was Stephen Decatur, who took his twenty-four pound guns onboard his ship while fighting the Barbary Pirates. Decatur made numerous trips to the iron works in the Barrens to personally supervise the work.

The numerous taverns in the Barrens were the home of politicians and travelers. Local candidates campaigned there and waited for the ballots to be counted. Weddings, as well as National Guard meetings, were held at these waystations.

During the American Revolution pirates roamed up and down the Barrens' inlets capturing over a thousand British ships and redistributing their precious cargos.

Today the towns that once bustled with the sound of iron on metal and the silent footsteps of smugglers carrying their bounty are long gone. But if one stands on the sandy paths of the Pine Barrens and listens carefully to the wind in the pines, the sounds of the past can still be heard, if only in the listener's imagination.

Adventure On The Jersey Shore

THE EARLY HISTORY of New Jersey was intricately linked to the sea, with the ocean providing a livelihood for the many people who lived along its rocky shores. The story of the South Jersey shore is rich in the history of 19th century America.

When the United States declared war against England in 1812, the first members of the New Jersey militia to go into battle were established in Egg Harbor and Navesink Highlands. They organized five companies and one artillery detachment to guard the shore against British attack. In time, a small fort was built at Great Egg Harbor that contained four and six pound cannons. Sailors from the nearby counties later moved to Sandy Hook to help protect New York Harbor.

But it was in Ocean County that the war became a personal battle. The British used the coast route to New York as their main waterway, attacking and seizing many vessels near Barnegat Inlet and Cape May. A favorite tactic of the British was to send a barge ashore to kill or capture cattle on the nearby farms.

Near Cape May, which was frequently raided, the Fishing Creek Salt Works were burned to the ground by a British man-of-war.

The shore counties saw the development of shipbuilding firsthand. In the years preceeding the American Revolution, a flourishing trade had developed. Whaleboats were constructed before the 1700's, the two most important being the *Clumsy* and the *Garvey*.

The residents of both Ocean and Atlantic counties depended heavily on the shipbuilding industry. At the turn of the 19th century, Tuckertown had five schooners under work at one time. Shipmasons, like the Bartlett family and Ebenezer Tucker, built countless ships just like a present-day car assembly plant. By 1850, the Atlantic County towns of Mays Landing and Tuckahoe became the industrial centers of the shore.

Joseph Francis, a Toms River native, built a rowboat in 1830 which he sent as a gift to the Russian Czar. The Czar later used it in the Cowes Regatta in England. Francis is also noted for creating an improved and more buoyant wooden lifeboat and, later, an enclosed lifeboat which proved very successful in rescuing shipwrecked passengers along the shoal-infested Jersey shore.

Another pioneer of Atlantic County was George May. May a shipbuilder and blacksmith, founded the town of Mays Landing and he answered the trust of the people by supplying the many schooners that berthed in Great Egg Harbor. From

1830 to 1880, over one hundred keels were laid at Mays Landing.

Red Bank served as the center of ship construction in Monmouth County. It was here that the ships were built for the route that connected Monmouth County and New York.

Salvage and lifesaving also played an important part in the early days of the ocean counties.

Countless ships ran aground near shore due to the inadequately marked shoals and reefs. Many wrecks occurred in the winter and fall when rough seas made navigating difficult.

A lifesaving unit was established along the coast from Barnegat City, north to Long Beach Island and then up into Long Island Sound to protect ships, which was the beginning of the Coast Guard as we know it today.

"Wreckers", people who collected goods from washed up ships, were scarce but a problem nevertheless.

In order to prevent the ever increasing incidents of death and destruction along the coast, the Congress authorized the construction of a number of lighthouses along the shore.

Beginning in 1761 and continuing to 1900, 15 lighthouses were built from Cape May, Barnegat, Long Beach and north to Sea Isle City.

The coming of the railroad in the 1850's saw the decline of the sea trade as the commercial backbone of the South Jersey shore.

But the lure of the sea will be felt as long as the waves pound and little boys dream.

Thomas Nicholson and His Days with the Barbary Pirates

AS A YOUNG lad in New Jersey in the early 1800's, Thomas Nicholson yearned to go to sea and view the world beyond his home.

While still in his teens, young Tom joined the Navy and left his home on an adventure that would take him around the world and into battle against the Barbary Pirates. His diary describes his adventures and his long imprisonment by the Barbary Pirates.

On January 3, 1809, Thomas Nicholson joined the Navy. After receiving basic training on board a large brig in Philadelphia, he set sail for the Mediterranean. His destination was the port of Algiers, where the American Navy was engaged in a battle against the Sultan of Algiers over shipping rights in that part of the world.

After a month's voyage, the ship sighted the white port of Algiers, along the Barbary Coast, home of the Barbary Pirates. Thomas observed that its towering minarets dominated the harbor. As the ship entered the Algerian port, it was attacked. After a short, intense battle, it was overpowered by the Algerian Navy.

Thomas Nicholson and 15 of his fellow seaman were taken prisoner. Little did he know that the day was to be the start of years of captivity, torture and isolation from his friends and family.

The prisoners were taken to meet the Dey of Algiers, the ruler of the Barbary kingdom. As they were paraded through the streets of Algiers, they were stoned by angry crowds that had lined up to watch them go by.

According to Nicholson's diary, the Dey was about 60 years old, had a long white beard and wore a traditional, flowing headdress. Shortly after his audience with the Dey, Nicholson and his fellow prisoners were paraded in the square of the city and auctioned off as slaves. Unlike some of his friends, Nicholson was lucky to have been bought by a man who showed some mercy towards him. He was taken to the owner's plantation where he worked digging ditches. Nicholson had no tools to work with and had to make do with large rocks and stones.

For years he suffered the humiliation of captivity. Yet he never lost faith and planned for his eventual escape. His first real opportunity came when he was taken, along with a group of other Americans, by his master to the city of Algiers.

Managing to cut their ropes, the survivors hit their owner over the head with a spade, bound him and pushed him into a deep well. They fled across the hot desert but only got five miles before being recaptured.

One of the group was publicly hanged for the escape

attempt but through the luck of the draw Nicholson was saved from the gallows.

For his punishment he wore around his neck a broad strip of hide which caused him to walk permanently face to the ground.

Two years later, with the strip finally off, and with his health once more regained, Nicholson had a second chance to escape.

Once again in the city of Algiers he and another prisoner were left at a market square while their owner went seeking goods for trade.

They cut their ropes and, wearing traditional Arab dress, made their way to the harbor where many foreign ships were docked.

They swam toward a European frigate in the harbor and were given protection.

The Dey's soldiers searched the ship but never found Tom and his companion, who were hidden in a water flask.

That day the ship left Algiers and returned to London, thus ending the almost ten year nightmare of young Thomas Nicholson.

New Jersey's Ex-King and the Crown Jewels

THE HISTORY OF New Jersey can be narrated with
the stories of the lives of many people who served their
country on the battlefield and in politics, but most people
don't know that New Jersey has also played host to an
ex-king, who became a resident of the Garden State.

In the early 1800's, Napoleon Bonaparte of France was
deposed as ruler of his country and was sent to the island of
Elba in disgrace. While in power, Bonaparte gave his brother
Joseph the title of King of Spain. When Napoleon fell from
power, so did his brother Joseph, who now found himself a
man without a crown.

Joseph and his family left Spain, just one step ahead of the law, for a safe haven in Switzerland. He decided to book passage to the United States, accompanied by a secretary, and disguised as an ordinary passenger. He took only a suitcase of jewels with him, deciding it was safer to bury the remainder, with his gold, on the grounds of his Swiss hideaway.

Looking for a place to stay, one that would measure up to his social class, Joseph settled near Bordentown on a stretch of wooded land he called Point Breeze.

Joseph's property consisted of over a thousand acres of forest with gardens and lawns beautifully placed for a splendid effect.

Bonaparte's Point Breeze home took three years to complete and when it was finished his two daughters came from Europe to live with their father.

But there was secret side to Joseph Bonaparte's Point Breeze home, one that never had a concrete explanation.

Perhaps fearing attack by agents of France's enemies, England or Spain, or Americans unfriendly to his cause, Joseph built a secret part to his home on the hill.

He constructed a tall outpost or belvedere which commanded a vast panorama of the adjoining countryside. Also built were underground passageways from the main house to other less travelled parts of the estate. The tunnels were fortified with brick and were high enough for people to walk through standing erect.

As time went on, Joseph wanted to recover his buried fortune. He turned to his secretary and friend, Louis Mailliard. Mailliard sailed to Europe from Philadelphia on August 22, 1817. He carried letters representing him to be Stephen Girard, a wealthy businessman. His trip proved to be a dangerous one from the start. His ship was wrecked off the coast of Ireland, but luckily he and the other passengers were rescued. He finally arrived in Europe and traveled overland to Switzerland, keeping an eye open for trouble.

He finally arrived in Switzerland at Joseph's hideaway

chateau. He found Monsieur Veret, Joseph's valet. In the darkness of night, the two went to the secret hiding place, and, much to their relief, found that the treasure remained. Placing many of the jewels in a reinforced belt that he wore around his waist and taking the rest of the gold on his person, Louis headed on to Brussels, Belgium.

In Brussels, Louis visited Joseph's wife, Queen Julie. Heeding her doctor's orders not to travel, she remained in Belgium. It was at that time that the couple's two daughters returned with Louis, to reside with their father in New Jersey. Louis Mailliard's five months of journey and danger ended and Joseph was reunited with his fabulous treasure at his Bordentown home.

As time went on the Emperor's brother began to receive guests. Not only did his Bordentown neighbors come to say hello and spend a quiet afternoon but other Americans, men who were household names, came to pay their respects. Among those who stopped at Point Breeze were John Quincy Adams, later to become the sixth President of the United States, and Henry Clay and Daniel Webster.

While Joseph Bonaparte never became a naturalized citizen of the United States, the New Jersey legislature passed a bill allowing him to own land, in effect making him a Jerseyman.

Joseph Bonaparte lived in Bordentown for 14 years. Later, he made a trip to England, returned to the United States and on his final journey went to Italy.

Thus ended the life of the first "king" of New Jersey.

The Lure of the Great Falls

FOR CENTURIES THE Great Falls of Paterson have lured thousands of people to view the majestic curtain of water cascade down a funnel of rocks, gathering speed as it hits the cliffs below.

The Falls have played a paramount part in the history of the Passaic Valley, surviving and bearing witness to the great events that shaped North Jersey history.

The Lenni Lenape Indians, probably the first people to see the Falls, called it "Totowa", which means "to sink or be forced down by weight."

Nobody knows exactly when the first settlers discovered the Great Falls but it can be assumed that when the settlement of Newark was founded in 1679 traders and trappers made their way to the Falls.

As the years passed, knowledge of the Falls became widespread. People carved their names or initials in the covering of the cliffs. Among those whose names were etched on the rocks is George Washington, whose troops stayed in the area during the Revolutionary War.

During the American Revolution the Godwin House was built near the Falls to accommodate the many travelers who made their way into the Passaic Valley.

The Falls proved to be a popular fishing region for both the Indians and the white settlers, who began to make permanent homes in the area. Shad and sturgeon were among the more popular fish in the waters of the Falls; numerous beaver traps dotted the river.

In 1791, vast improvements in the physical nature of the Falls took place.

A group called The Society For Useful Manufactures led the improvements. Among the construction projects done at the Falls were the building of a raceway and the fashioning of many mills and workshops at the base of the Falls. The highlight of the improvements was the creation of a four-and-one-half foot dam that was secured to the boulders in the riverbed.

The dam provided steam through the raceway which in turn provided three canals with power. The dam adjusted the amount of water from the Falls, lowering the quantity by means of guard gates.

The city of Paterson reaped the financial rewards that the power of the Falls provided. Numerous businesses opened and for a time the city was the industrial rival of New York.

One of the early pioneers who brought his business to Paterson was Sam Colt. Colt built his gun mill, a four story building with a weather vane in the shape of a gun, near the Great Falls. Colt made various guns with silver and gold handles and sold them not only to Americans but to foreign princes and heads of state as well.

In 1827, Timothy Crane built a bridge over the Falls and named it after De Witt Clinton, Governor of New York. The bridge was held upright by curved supports that spread out from the middle of the Falls. By the time the United States entered World War I, five bridges had been built over the Falls.

As the Falls became more popular it was inevitable that tragedies would take place.

Among those who died in accidents at the Falls were Sarah Cumming, the wife of a Newark minister, who slipped on a ledge and William Whitaker, a sailor, who fell off a pole at the southern end of the Falls.

During the War of 1812 the city of Paterson really came into its own. The cut-off of British goods to the United States was the stimulus that the area needed and American ingenuity took over.

Among the industrial pioneers who set up shop in Paterson were John Colt, who invented cotton duck sail, George Murray and John Ryle, who introduced the manufacture of silk to Paterson, John Holland, who built the first operational submarine, and Thomas Rogers, a builder of locomotives.

The Society for Useful Manufactures, the industrial society first organized in 1791 by Alexander Hamilton, went out of business in 1945.

All the pioneers of the Great Falls district are gone but if one stands on the rock ledge and listens to the roar of the water below, the ghosts of time past can still be heard, if only in one's imagination.

New Jersey's Privateers

THE REVOLUTIONARY WAR in New Jersey wasn't fought on land alone. More dramatic battles took place on the many waterways of our state that lead to the trade routes of the Atlantic.

The men of New Jersey who fought the British as privateers owned their own ships, armed them with their own funds and carried a license or letter of marque that legally allowed them to prey on the enemy, in this case the armed British ships that sailed the coasts.

Our New Jersey privateers made a good living at their dangerous job, sometimes making a thousand dollars on one cruise and sharing the profits from a captured vessel.

These brave seamen were so instrumental in sinking and capturing British men-of-war that it was estimated by one member of the British Parliament that from the years 1776 to 1778 over 733 ships worth $10,000,000 were lost.

By 1780, the ranks of the New Jersey and other privateers operating along the Atlantic seaboard totaled over 450 ships armed with 7,000 guns. Between 1776 and 1780, they had captured or destroyed some 1,200 British ships.

The Toms River and New Brunswick areas were also the scenes of many sea battles between the British and the American privateers.

Captain Sam Bigelow was one of the most capable of all the pilots in the region.

He had a string of good luck in 1780, taking the British schooner *Betsey* at Long Beach Island, loaded with supplies for English soldiers in New York. In the winter of 1780, Bigelow nabbed another British ship, the *Dove,* that followed a wrong course and also wound up near Long Beach. The English captain, thinking that he was on Long Island, New York, sent a boat to shore looking for supplies. Instead, the unlucky sailors walked right into Bigelow's arms.

The climatic battle against the New Jersey privateers came on September 30, 1778 when a British convoy of nine ships and three hundred men left New York for Little Neck Harbor.

The British arrived off shore on October 5, but the Americans had advance notice and, despite a massacre of fifty men from General Pulaski's troops on Osborne Island, the privateers did not suffer the loss of a single ship.

In the heyday of privateering in New Jersey, the town of Chestnut Neck at Little Egg Harbor became the headquarters for anti-British raids. The land around Chestnut Neck was perfect for staging attacks against the enemy, owing to the difficult channels and sand bars that guarded the shore and small inlets that were a natural sanctuary for ships.

One of the most daring New Jersey privateers of the day was Captain Adam Hyler of New Brunswick. Hyler operated near the Sandy Hook Lighthouse, which was in waters controlled by huge British warships that guarded the entrance to that southern port.

In daring raids in which Hyler used sailboats and heavily armed whaleboats manned by master oarsmen, he'd lure British vessels into sight and then attack with cannon, surprising the enemy ship. In one day in 1781, Captain Hyler is credited with attacking five British ships near Sandy Hook and, after a fifteen minute battle, capturing or disabling all of them.

It is of some note that this adventurous sailor died quietly in bed of natural causes in 1782, one year after his amazing victory.

The Griggstown Spy

THROUGHOUT THE HISTORY of battle, nations have employed spies to reconnoiter behind enemy lines and report back all the information they've collected.

One such spy, originally from England but who went over to the colonial side during the American Revolution, provided significant intelligence in an important battle in New Jersey that turned the tide of the conflict in favor of the United States.

John Honeyman, a Scotch-Irishman, was drafted into the British army and came to America in 1758 with the forces under Colonel Wolf to fight the French in Canada.

During a battle, Honeyman survived an attack on his boat

in which the officer seated next to him was killed, climbed the Heights of Abraham in Quebec and was responsible for carrying the dead body of his commander, now General Wolf, from the killing ground.

One year after the war ended, John Honeyman went to the new American colonies, first settling in Philadelphia where he married and later moving to Griggstown in Somerset.

When the Americans revolted against British rule, Honeyman took the colonial side, and, using letters given to him by his late commander, General Wolf, attesting to his military competence, made contact with General Washington. In Fort Lee, where Washington was encamped, the two men met. Honeyman presented his papers and he was accepted as a spy by the fledgling army.

The plan that George Washington and John Honeyman concocted was both audacious and fraught with danger.

There were many Tories (British sympathizers) in New Jersey and it was decided that the ex-British soldier was to cross over into his former countrymen's lines, and, posing as a butcher, learn all he could about the activities in the enemy camp.

As soon as Honeyman found any vital information he was to cross to the nearest American outpost, where he'd be captured. General Washington gave standing orders that a reward was to be paid for the capture of the spy and that he shouldn't be harmed.

Bringing his cattle south, he went to Trenton and openly entered the city and set up shop. He traded with the British but on his trips across the city he observed the condition of the enemy. He discovered that the British forces in town were a lax state owing partially to the winter and he also mapped out all the roads into and out of Trenton.

With his information in hand, he left the city and traveled to the nearest American line. He was instantly recognized by the colonial Army. He taunted them until they gave chase and captured him; he was taken to General Washington's headquarters.

Honeyman spent a half hour alone with the General, imparted his knowledge and was taken to the stockade. That night a fire near the camp was set and the guards watching Honeyman went to put it out. When they returned the prisoner had vanished into the night.

Three days after the escape of John Honeyman, Washington's troops crossed the Delaware, stormed the British garrison at Trenton and scored one of the most vital victories of the war.

But John Honeyman also served his commander with another important act. Following his jailbreak and previous to Washington's attack on Trenton, he returned to his British friends. He told them that the Americans were underfed, their army was small and untrained and their morale was low. Thus he deceived the British into thinking Washington's troops were weaker than they were.

Honeyman's reputation as an authentic American hero followed him home and, while some of the townspeople at Griggstown disliked him for his apparent ties to the British, he was treated with the respect due a man who unselfishly served his adopted country.

Revolutionary War Battles along the Jersey Coast

WHEN ONE THINKS of the important battles of the American Revolution, the campaigns of Trenton, Princeton and Morristown instantly come to mind. Often overlooked are the battles and scrimmages of the Revolution which took place along the New Jersey coastal area.

In the late 1700s, when the United States declared its independence from England, the Jersey shore was the main shipbuilding and commercial center of the state. It was here that ships loaded with trade goods stopped for unloading and for reshipment to New York and Philadelphia.

The British, as well as the colonists, knew the strategic

37

importance of the Jersey coastal area, and their battle plans reflected that knowledge.

The town of Tuckertown was the main seaport on the South Jersey shore. Its most important industries were lumbering and shipbuilding. During the American Revolution, at least 30 ships at a time were berthed in Tuckertown. It was from these bustling docks that the colonists raided many ships that were enroute to New York.

In one of the most adventurous actions of the war, which brought the wrath of the British down upon the Americans, two English ships were captured off Sandy Hook.

The two unfortunate British merchantmen, the *Venus* and the *Major Pearson* were taken to the busy docks at Tuckertown where they were stripped of their cargos.

In response, Governor General Clinton vowed to wipe out the sailors at Chestnut Neck and Tuckertown.

In the fall of 1778, 700 British troops sailed south, with Tuckertown as their final destination.

But colonial intelligence had spotted the ships as they left New York and word of their departure reached General Washington who immediately ordered the fleet at Tuckertown to leave at once.

General Washington sent the Polish General Count Casimir Pulaski, to defend Tuckertown against the impending British attack.

As the British troops advanced, they burned Chestnut Neck on the Mullica River, destroyed 12 houses at Bass River and burned down Thankers Mill. British soldiers then landed on Osborn's Island, four miles from Tuckertown, and captured an American soldier who led them to General Pulaski's headquarters.

The Polish General and his men were pursued across the beach and marshes and by the time the battle ended, 30 men had been killed.

But General Pulaski's men showed their skill and bravery

and managed to ground the British ship *Zebra*, and sailed it back to a jubilant crowd at Tuckertown.

If Tuckertown was the commercial center of the Jersey shore, then Long Beach Island served as the perfect hiding place for American sailors and soldiers.

They lured many British men-of-war into the tiny inlets and captured large cargos of food and guns.

Not all Americans served the Revolution. One who didn't was John Bacon, the most notorious pirate on the shore. He was a renegade who was responsible for killings at Manahawkin and other shore points. As Bacon's reputation grew, the Governor of New Jersey put a price on his head of 50 pounds.

On October 25, 1782, a British cutter bound for St. Thomas in the Virgin Islands ran aground at the Barnegat shoals.

She was pursued and captured by the American ship *Alligator* under the command of Captain Andrew Steelman of Cape May.

But one of the crewmen of the British ship managed to escape during the confusion of the battle and made his way to the camp of John Bacon.

Bacon then gathered up his men and put to sea in their boat called the *Hero's Revenge*.

Bacon landed his troops at night on the beach where the crew of the *Alligator* were sleeping and out of a contingent of 25, five escaped death.

Thus ended the so-called Long Beach Massacre at the hands of the Jersey Shore's most wanted pirate.

Elias Boudinot, America's First President

<hr>
<hr>

IF SOMEONE TOLD you that George Washington wasn't the first president of the United States you would probably look a little startled. If you were interested you'd probably ask: "Who then was the father of our country?" If you were told, "Elias Boudinot," you'd probably ask, "Who?"

Of the many historical figures from the Revolutionary War period the name and accomplishments of Elias Boudinot aren't widely known. But he played a major role in the creation of the United States and worked side by side with the many founding fathers who actively sought his advice.

Who was Elias Boudinot and what role did he play in the making of the United States?

Elias Boudinot came from Newark, the son of French Huguenots. After spending his formative years in Newark, he moved to Philadelphia and was a neighbor of Benjamin Franklin. His family later came back to New Jersey where Elias studied law and religion.

As a young man he joined the Whig party, whose members believed that government should protect property.

As he saw the repressive policies of the British government in the Thirteen Colonies, he knew that something would have to be done to change the explosive political situation. But like other men of property, he was a reluctant supporter of the British and knew that time was not on their side.

As the British sent more soldiers to America and resentment toward their rule grew stronger, Boudinot entered the political arena. Following the Boston Tea Party, he was elected by the leaders of New Jersey to the Committees of Correspondence, which called for a union of all the colonies.

As the fighting intensified between the colonists and the British, Boudinot served as a delegate to the Provincial Congress and worked secretly to get ammunition for General Washington's new army.

Elias Boudinot's first official post in the revolutionary struggle was as commissary of prisoners of the Continental Army. Elias had a difficult task as the new commissioner, as he had to deal fairly with the hundreds of British prisoners that were in colonial jails. He had to oversee their care, provide food, shelter and arrange prisoner-of-war exchanges.

He also had the job of making sure that the Americans held by the British were well treated. That the British considered Americans to be traitors didn't help the situation at all.

If Boudinot had problems with the prison system, he had an even more difficult problem in gaining the necessary money to fund the new department. The Continental Congress refused to spend the necessary funds and he had to use his own money to buy supplies for both British and American prisoners.

In August 1780, he stepped down from his position and returned to private life. But his self-imposed isolation was only temporary and in 1781 he was elected to a seat in the Continental Congress, a move that would have a profound effect in his later life.

The Congress that Elias served in was now the main governmental body of the newly declared colonies. The delegates had adopted the Articles of Confederation, the body of law that set down how the country was to be governed.

The first controversy that Boudinot was involved in was the disposition of the vast western lands beyond the Ohio River.

A few of the large states laid claims to these largely uncharted lands, but did little to settle them. New Jersey wanted the western lands to be incorporated into the nation as a whole. Elias Boudinot was one of those who saw in the western lands a vast new source of wealth for the United States and did all he could to make them part of the country. He, along with other men, formed the Miami Associates to take as much of the western lands as possible. They formed the New Jersey Land Society and asked the Continental Congress for the right to buy two million acres of land between the Mississippi and the Au Vase rivers. But the deal fell through, leaving Elias and his friends on their own. Boudinot and another New Jerseyan, Jonathan Dayton, established the East Jersey Company for the purpose of buying two million acres on the Little Miami River, but this project, like the Miami Associates, never got off the ground.

His new stature in the western lands debate made him a powerful political figure. When the members of the Continental Congress gathered to choose a president, they elected Elias Boudinot as the new chief executive. Thus, Elias Boudinot was in effect, the "first president of the United States."

He also took over the job of acting minister of Foreign

Affairs and actively led negotiations for a treaty of friendship with Sweden. The establishment of diplomatic relations with Sweden proved to bring a bonus. When the new Swedish envoy arrived in the United States, he brought with him the news that Great Britain had agreed to a treaty ending the war with the colonies.

Boudinot moved the capital of the new republic, temporarily, to Nassau Hall. There, in Princeton, he effectively ran the country. But the ending of the war brought new challenges to his desk. The first was the fight over the establishment of a new United States Bank.

Boudinot's protegé and friend, Alexander Hamilton, was the man responsible for the creation of the new bank. In May of 1789, Boudinot proposed in Congress the creation of the bank, with Alexander Hamilton as its chief. Boudinot's bill provided for this official to have broad powers. He would assume responsibility for the collection of debts and the expenditures of the country.

Additionally, Boudinot sided with Hamilton against James Madison. James Madison wanted to end the national debt by attempting a profitable acquisition of western lands.

Boudinot said that the debt was still due and had to be paid off, regardless of the acquisition of the western lands.

In 1794, President Washington appointed Boudinot as director of the U.S. Mint, an agency newly created and already in political hot water. Elias recommended that all the tools for the machinery of the Mint be produced in the United States instead of in Europe. He settled another controversy over the distribution of copper cents. A number of states complained that they could not get enough copper cents, as most of these coins went to a relative of Boudinot's, U.S. Treasurer Benjamin Rush, who gave most of these coins to Philadelphia banks only. Boudinot overruled Rush and ordered the Treasury to provide wide distribution throughout the country. He served for ten years as head of the Mint and turned it into a first-rate department.

After he retired from public life, he wrote of the important events of the day and made the adjustment from public figure to private citizen.

Elias Boudinot died peacefully on October 24, 1821, in his 81st year.

During his life he was overshadowed by Washington, Jefferson, Franklin and the other founding fathers, but Elias Boudinot played his own unique role in the early life of the United States.

The Court Martial of Benedict Arnold

THE TRIAL OF Benedict Arnold, one of the most notorious traitors in the history of the United States, took place in New Jersey at the end of the Revolutionary War.

Like other men who, for one reason or another, turn their backs on their country, Benedict Arnold was an early patriot.

At 15 he left home and fought in the Indian wars.

When the war against the British began in earnest in the Thirteen Colonies, Benedict Arnold took up arms once more.

When he was 35, he was sent to Fort Ticonderoga in New York, where he fought bravely against the British who were sweeping across New York. Later, he was transferred north to Quebec, Canada, where he led skirmishes against the British.

At the important battle of Saratoga, Arnold was wounded and suffered a shattered leg. The battle of Saratoga was important military in that it led to the surrender of British General Burgoyne and was a turning point in the Revolution.

By June 1778, the British had evacuated Philadelphia and were pursued by Washington's troops. It was during this lull in the battle that General Washington appointed Arnold commander of American forces in Philadelphia.

This was a safe posting for Arnold, who would be able to recover from his wounds.

During his stay in Philadelphia, Arnold, now recovering, married Margaret Shippen, a debutant with connections to the right people in that city. After their marriage they bought a home on the Schuykill.

But it was during this time of relative inactivity in Philadelphia that Arnold turned his attention to other, less lofty matters.

Arnold roamed the city making undesirable contacts. It was during this period that his political philosophy began to change. Using his title of Commander of American Forces in Philadelphia, Arnold began to abuse his office. He used soldiers under his nod to do menial tasks at his home, used government-owned wagons to bring supplies to the Tories, allowed a Tory ship to enter the port without reporting the fact, and, in a final affront, refused to explain his actions to the ruling Council of Pennsylvania.

When his superiors learned of his underground activities they called for an investigation.

But Arnold went one step further and demanded a court martial to clear his name.

In June 1780, before his trial and after his convert dealings, Arnold began corresponding with Sir Henry Clinton, the British Governor General in America.

What personal motives Arnold had in his secret writings with the British General are still unclear, even with the passage of time. Could it be that he had always been a British sympathizer? Or had he been bribed into changing his political attitudes?

The trial began on December 22, 1779, at the Taproom of Dickersons Tavern in Morristown.

Facing Arnold were three brigadier generals, Henry Knox, William Maxwell and Mordecai Gest, and eight colonels. The prosecutor was William Lawrence.

To his trial Arnold brought letters of reference from General Washington, who wrote of Arnold's courage.

In addressing the court in his defense, Arnold said that the charges against him were circumstantial and demanded that his prosecutors bring evidence against him for all the world to see.

On January 26, 1780, the military court convened. It found Arnold innocent but asked General Washington to issue a harsh reprimand. This was done.

After the trial Arnold accepted the post of Commander of West Point, one of the biggest mistakes Washington was to make.

Later that year, when Arnold was in command of the U.S. Military Academy, he offered to hand over West Point to the British in return for safe passage out of the country.

But his treasonous behavior was nipped in the bud and his plans fell through.

But if Arnold was lucky, the fates weren't as kind to his co-conspirator, Major John André, who was captured behind the American lines dressed in civilian clothes. Major André was shot as a spy.

Benedict Arnold fled to England where he lived out the rest of his life, his name forever etched in the shadowy history of our country.

William Franklin—New Jersey's Rouge Governor

THE OLD SAYING, "like father like son," certainly could not be more applicable than it is in the case of William Franklin and his famous father, Benjamin Franklin. Though they ended up on opposite sides of the Revolutionary cause, they were both men who remained highly partisan and rigid in support of their causes. One wonders how these two men of the same blood could arrive at such opposite beliefs.

William was the son of Benjamin Franklin and his common law wife. "Young Bill," as he was called, had an adventurous spirit that took him away from his native Philadelphia. With his father's blessing, William left home in

1740. For the next eight years, he set out to find himself in the new frontiers of the American West.

He joined the Pennsylvania Company and went to Albany to fight the French, who, in the mid-1700s, had come to the United States to seek new trade routes. Gaining experience in battle, William then moved on to the wild Ohio country as an assistant to an Indian trader called Conrad Weiser.

In his contacts with the Indians and the settlers in the Ohio Valley, young William learned valuable lessons in diplomacy that he would later use as governor.

After years of exploring the new territories, he returned to Philadelphia and became the city's postmaster.

William left Philadelphia and went to England as a member of the Pennsylvania Assembly. There he helped to mediate a dispute with the Penn family over taxation of proprietary lands they owned.

Franklin's influence on his son was overpowering and the ever willing son obeyed his father's orders. Franklin wanted his son to be a lawyer and William studied under a Philadelphia attorney named Joseph Galloway. When Franklin was elected to the Pennsylvania Legislature, William succeeded him as Clerk of the Assembly. When Franklin rounded up horses and wagons for General Braddock's ill-fated campaign against the French in 1755, William went along as his chief agent.

William's stay in London was an education in itself. He met and studied the people in power in England and made many political contacts.

But by 1760 he had returned home to begin one of the most important parts of his career.

Like his father, William sired an illegitimate son, William Temple. Grandfather Franklin understood his son's behavior and doted on the child. Two years later, on September 4, 1762, he married Elizabeth Downs of London.

Five days after his marriage William Franklin was sworn in as Governor of New Jersey.

His appointment was not taken lightly by the political watchers in the colony. Many people in government considered him unfit for the job because he had no experience and, to a lesser degree, because of his own illegitimacy.

William and his friends countered by highlighting his experience as a member of the Pennsylvania Assembly, his knowledge of military affairs and his influential friends in both the colonies and England. He was liked by the people of New Jersey and often visited their towns and listened to their complaints.

But where William deviated from his father was in his loyalty to the British crown, which had appointed him to office.

At the beginning of the British occupation of the colonies, William was directly confronted with the will of his constituents. He reluctantly carried out the Stamp Acts, which imposed taxes on goods, and he actively worked to stem the tide of revolution by sending news of the independence movement to London.

He was also the head of the Associated Loyalists, a pro-British party that conducted guerrilla war against the colonies.

But William was lucky as governor because New Jersey was spared the bitter internal turmoil of the other colonies. William blamed his partners in government for his troubles. At one point he had a heated argument with William Coxe, the provincial stamp distributor, who, as a trusted advisor, didn't tell the governor how to deal with the bad publicity surrounding the Stamp Act, which Coxe had to execute. Franklin's performance during the Stamp Act crisis was the result of his inexperience and ignorance of British colonial politics.

In 1775, Ben Franklin parted from his son. They were not to meet again until the war was over.

Back in New Jersey, William took on another domestic enemy, the Presbyterians. He wanted to take control of their main institution, the College of New Jersey at Princeton.

When they refused to relinquish control, William got a charter from the legislature to open in New Brunswick a competing school called Queen's College, later called Rutgers.

With American resistance stiffening and Franklin's motives now openly challenged, the people of New Jersey took action against him.

On January 8, 1776, he was captured in Perth Amboy. In July he was sent to jail in Lebanon, Connecticut, and three years later was exchanged for John McKinley, the former president of Delaware.

October 1778 found William living in British-occupied New York City where he worked to suppress the rebellion.

On September 18, 1782, 20 years after being appointed governor of New Jersey, he set sail for England and permanent exile.

Ben Franklin never forgave the wayward son who had so dishonored his family.

Some people called William Franklin a traitor, others called him a patriot. We will never be sure which, patriot or traitor, he felt himself to be.

New Jersey's Famous Duel

NEW JERSEY PLAYED an important part in the settlement of the United States with many significant events taking place here in the early days of the new nation.

But one incident between two of America's early pioneers in democracy, Aaron Burr and Alexander Hamilton, remains to this day a sad chapter in the life of our country and this state.

The presidential election of 1801 was one of the bitterest contests in the nation's history. Among many contenders for the presidency were Aaron Burr and Thomas Jefferson, both men of high standing in the new United States.

In the end, Jefferson won the election when the vote was

sent to the House of Representatives. Aaron Burr, humiliated by his loss, but still seeking his own power base, was chosen Vice President.

While the House debate was going on, the Federalist Party, led by Alexander Hamilton and Governor Morris, among others, held the balance of power in their hands. Those favoring both Jefferson and Burr courted the Federalists, with many promises being made on all sides.

In the course of the campaign, the Federalists themselves became divided, with a faction favoring Burr of the members led by Representative Bayard of Delaware.

Alexander Hamilton, one of the Federalist leaders, was angered at the way his party was sacrificing its principles in order to assure its political ends.

Hamilton wrote scathing letters to Representative Bayard, Governor Morris and others, asking them not to make a political pact with his arch-rival, Burr.

Hamilton called Burr an unscrupulous schemer, a man without political morality who would do anything to achieve his own ends.

With Jefferson's election, Burr became his vice-president, and, like many of the men who would follow him in that office, became quickly bored with the position.

In 1805, Burr decided to run for governor of New York, beating Morgan Lewis who was publicly supported by Alexander Hamilton.

It was during Burr's campaign for governor that his dispute with Hamilton reached its climax.

Hamilton, it was reported in the local press, spoke so harshly against Burr that the Governor sought revenge. Saying that Hamilton had defamed him, Burr challenged Hamilton to a duel.

Under the strict rules governing duels, both protagonists had their seconds plan the event. Burr chose William Van Ness, a twenty-six-year-old lawyer and personal friend. Hamilton's second was Nathaniel Pendleton, a fifty-eight-year-old lawyer, a former officer in the American Revolution.

Their duel took place on a July morning on a thin strip of land on the New Jersey side of the Palisades near Weehawken.

Both men squared off and, after they turned and fired their pistols, Hamilton lay mortally wounded. He was taken by boat across the Hudson to New York City where he died in a house at the present 82 Jane Street in Lower Manhattan.

After the duel, Burr, having been notified that he was wanted on murder charges, fled the state.

He first went to Perth Amboy, crossed the Delaware to Pennsylvania, took flight to the safety of St. Simons Island off the Georgia coast and finally took refuge at the plantation home of Harman Blennerhasset, an old friend.

Later he returned to Washington only to find that he was a political outcast in the nation's capital.

With his political career in ruins, Aaron Burr fled west with the hope of forming his own army to take Louisiana away from the United States.

Burr's travels through the West and his constant talk of taking up arms against the United States were two of the more controversial aspects of his life.

Despite the fact that Burr and Hamilton will always be remembered for their duel on the banks of the Hudson, it should be noted that they should also be remembered for the major roles they played in the creation of the United States.

The Legacy of Aaron Burr

ONE OF THE most controversial figures in American history, Aaron Burr, grew up in New Jersey. Burr was vice president of the United States under Thomas Jefferson and is most remembered for the duel on the cliffs of Weehawken in which he killed Alexander Hamilton.

But why did this graduate of Princeton University turn his attention away from the country he loved? And were the charges leveled against him by his countrymen justified?

Aaron Burr's troubles and the beginning of his secret adventures followed the duel in which he killed Alexander Hamilton. With warrants out for his arrest in both New Jersey and New York, the former Vice President fled south, first stopping in Washington, D.C. and then going to the plantation home at St. Simons Island, Georgia of his friend Harman Blennerhasset.

Vice President Burr saw the new United States as a country in transition, one that needed lands in the unexplored West to enlarge the nation.

But the areas of interest to Burr were owned by Spain and there was little likelihood that Spain would give up her possessions without a fight.

To Burr's mind, the people of the West, mainly Louisiana and Texas, had no loyalty to the United States. They were Spanish subjects who had little in common with the government in Washington D.C.

Burr envisioned a plan, developed with Harman Blennerhasset and General of the Army James Wilkinson, to dismember those territories in the West and create a new nation of which he would be the leader.

By 1805 Burr had traveled to the West and recruited men and supplies for his venture. Harman Blennerhasset financed the plan and General Wilkinson oversaw the military training.

But unknown to Burr, his partner General Wilkinson was secretly working for the Spanish Minister to the United States, Yruyo, giving him information about Burr's plans. Wilkinson came to be known as "Agent No. 13."

While the former Vice President was widely liked in the West, the newspapers took a critical look at his adventures. As he traveled, people with whom he'd come in contact reported his plans, and the papers, especially *The Aurora*, called for an investigation.

In the publicity Burr's expedition came to be known as the "conspiracy."

Another critical event in the so-called "conspiracy" was the "cipher letter," supposedly written by Burr, outlining the seizure of Spanish lands.

The high points of the cipher letter were the following; Burr was to be in charge, with General Wilkinson as his deputy, the British navy would send ships to meet Burr's forces at the Mississippi and then they would decide if a strike against Baton Rouge was necessary.

The author of this version of the cipher letter, however, was not Aaron Burr but his friend, Jonathan Dayton, although Burr did write a different letter detailing his plans.

With public attention now shifting from Burr, he fled into the wilds of western Mississippi, aided by his last friends and colleagues.

Back in Washington, Burr's one time partner, General Wilkinson, betrayed him while hiding his own part in the plot.

While encamped at a creek near the town of Chester, South Carolina, Burr was captured and taken back to Richmond, Virginia for trial.

The presiding judge at his trial was the Chief Justice of the Supreme Court, John Marshall. Marshall, after reading all the pre-trial material, agreed to charge Burr with the crime of high misdemeanor. Treason had not been proven and that charge was dropped.

While the government tried to prove its case, many of its star witnesses never showed up and when they did, their testimony proved faulty. After weeks of waiting, the court finally heard from General Wilkinson. He shouldn't have appeared.

After reviewing the famous cipher letter, the jury decided that Wilkinson had doctored it to hide his own participation (which he did) and he was indicted.

In the end Burr was acquitted of the charges.

He spent a considerable amount of time in Europe, trying unsuccessfully to gain support for an attack on the Spanish lands in the United States.

He returned to New York and after a short illness died at the age of 80. Aaron Burr is buried at the Princeton Cemetery.

The Raritan Steamboat Wars

TODAY THE RARITAN River slowly moves down its curving path with the occasional speedboat plying its historic waters. The once heavily traveled cowpaths are still, save for the occasional hiker out for a day's walk.

But it wasn't always so quiet on the old river that runs through the central part of New Jersey.

During the mid-18th century, the Raritan River was the scene of a power struggle between New York and New Jersey for the commercial and navigation rights to the river.

The battle between the two states began with the development of the steamboat by Robert Fulton and John Fitch. These two early pioneers of the steam trade were given the sole right of navigation on New York waterways. Their rival was the Stevens family of Hoboken who built their own steamboat, the *Phoenix,* in 1806, which carried freight and passengers.

With the monopoly of passage on the New York route given to Fulton, Fitch, and, later, Robert Livingston, the *Phoenix* had its corner of New Jersey to itself.

The Steven's *Phoenix* plied the waters between Hoboken and New Brunswick, black smoke pouring from her stack, giving Fulton and Company stiff competition.

Fulton didn't take the Stevens's challenge lying down. He put the *Raritan* into service between New York and New Brunswick. Fulton's *Raritan* charged one third the price the *Phoenix* charged and saved passengers the trouble of ferrying to and from New York if they went on the *Phoenix* to Hoboken. The steamboat wars had begun.

The battle between the two states grew even hotter as the New Jersey Legislature passed a law that said that any Jersey skipper whose boats were captured in the waters of New York could take any New York ship found on the Jersey side.

The decision by the New Jersey Legislature hurt the state's own traffic as much as that of New York. Jersey skippers virtually stopped their runs on the Raritan for fear of losing their boats, their only source of income.

With a stalemate in the making and tempers flaring in both Trenton and Albany, a new element entered the case, one that was to have consequences far beyond the local dispute.

In 1819, Thomas Gibbons, a wealthy planter from Savannah, Georgia and now a resident of New Jersey, entered the steamboat war. He sent his own boat, the *Bellona,* on a route between New Brunswick and New York. Gibbons's main competition was a New York schooner called the *Olive Branch.* In his fight with the *Olive Branch,* Gibbons promised that his boat would beat his rival by two hours sailing time and his fare would be half that of the other steamboat.

With Gibbons's entry into the steamboat wars, the conflict

now took an entirely different course, one that would have profound effects on the commerce of the United States for years to come.

Gibbons took the case against the monopoly headed by Fulton and his partners, John Fitch and Robert Livingston, to the Supreme Court of the United States.

Gibbons's lawyer was none other than Daniel Webster, one of the most respected lawyers in the country.

Arguing before Chief Justice John Marshall, Webster swayed the court in Gibbons's favor. In their opinion, the justices said that in matters of interstate commerce between two states, the federal law had to be upheld over local state law.

This major decision by the Supreme Court granted the federal government the power to regulate commerce and navigation between states. This was the first major conflict in the states rights versus federal control dilemma that is still with us today.

The Court's decision was a boon to river traffic on the Raritan.

It seemed that scores of steamboats sprang up overnight on the river. Water traffic was so heavy that the waterway had to be enlarged to keep ahead of the congestion.

In 1832, construction began on the Delaware and Raritan Canal. Gangs of immigrant laborers were brought in from New York to dig the huge ditches needed to build the canal. The workers fought exhaustion, a cholera epidemic, extreme cold and heat, but by 1834, the canal was finished.

Another casualty of the river wars was John Fitch, one of the main actors in the conflict. Long before the completion of the Delaware and Raritan Canal, Fitch, broke and dispirited, fled to Kentucky. He tried to make the waters of the Mississippi another haven for river traffic. But he failed and, in June of 1798, he committed suicide.

Robert Stockton—New Jersey Trailblazer

NEW JERSEY HAS sent many of her citizens to do battle in the service of her country.

One of the most distinguished was a naval captain from Princeton, Robert Stockton.

Robert Stockton was born in 1795, the grandson of Richard Stockton, one of the signers of the Declaration of Independence.

In the early 1800s, Robert Stockton left his home in Princeton and joined the newly established United States Navy. After training he was given a commission and was sent to do battle against the Barbary Pirates in the Mediterranean.

His first command was as skipper of the ship *Spitfire.* At the helm of the ship, Stockton captured an Algerian man-of-war, leading his sailors onboard the enemy ship and putting her out of action.

Stockton's heroism was noted by his superiors and, in 1821, after serving with the Navy in Gibralter, Stockton was sent on another mission to Africa on behalf of the United States Government and the Colonization Society.

His job was to negotiate a treaty with the African rulers to set aside a colony on the west coast of Africa to be the new home of freed American slaves.

Sailing on the warship *Alligator,* Stockton conducted extensive and difficult talks with many of the native rulers who did not take kindly to American intrusion in their sovereign territory. Stockton had trouble especially with Chief Peter, who refused to agree to give up any land. Stockton, through threats, intimidation and a little forceful persuasion, made the Chief see things his way. The result of his efforts was the founding of Liberia the first colony for former slaves, who could live there in freedom.

Captain Stockton was also instrumental in capturing slave ships in the West Indies and in breaking up the lucrative slave trade in the Americas.

On his way home, he attacked Portuguese ships and was court martialed by the top Navy brass. It was only through the good offices of Daniel Webster, who interceded on his behalf, that Stockton was spared further punishment.

In 1823 Robert Stockton married Marie Potter of Charleston, South Carolina.

Five years later, looking for a life other than that of naval officer, Robert and his father-in-law, a wealthy businessman, began to finance the proposed Raritan Canal in his native state of New Jersey.

In 1841, he built the first steam-powered ship used by the Navy. His vessel, named the *Princeton,* was a new design with the machinery and engines built inside the ship, below the water line. The *Princeton* also had on deck two wrought-iron guns which carried a 225 pound shot.

On the *Princeton* Stockton would taste disaster. On February 28, 1844, President Tyler and his cabinet boarded the *Princeton* to inspect the ship's guns. After repeated successful tests, one more demonstration was ordered. As the powerful gun fired, one of the cannons exploded, killing the Secretary of State, the Secretary of the Navy and President Tyler's father-in-law.

But Robert Stockton's role in history was finally clinched by his actions in California.

When the United States and Mexico went to war in 1846, Stockton, then in California, joined forces with Lieutenant Colonel John C. Fremont and captured Los Angeles from the Mexicans.

Stockton appointed Fremont governor of the newly liberated territory and took on the title of "Conqueror of California."

Robert Stockton, the Jerseyman from Princeton who helped capture California for the United States ended his public career as senator from New Jersey.

A Jerseyman's Search For Gold

WHAT DOES NEW Jersey have to do with the California Gold Rush of 1848?

Nothing on the surface, but if one digs deeper one will find some interesting facts concerning one of the most exciting periods in American history.

The discovery of gold in California took place in 1848 in the rugged territory of the Sacramento Valley. The "Forty-Niners" came like a pack of wild dogs to this cold, desolate place, searching for the vast amount of gold that lay buried beneath the rocks and in the crystal-clear streams in the high Sierras.

But it was a New Jersey native, James Marshall of Lambertville, who discovered the first gold nugget and set off the California gold rush.

Who was this man who helped to make history and what was his story?

James Marshall was born in Lambertville in 1810 and lived in New Jersey until the age of 21.

Ever eager to see the world and growing restless with his limited future at home, he headed west at the age of 21, seeking a new life.

He crossed the desolate plains, struggling to keep alive as he met the new, vast America beyond the East.

Marshall's first stop of any permanence was Missouri, where he set up shop, but his health began to fail and upon his doctor's advice, he went further west to the golden coast of California.

After a treacherous journey across the West he finally made it to the Sacramento Valley before the summer of 1845 and settled at Sutter's Fort.

Sutter's Fort was the way station for those people crossing the country into California. The fort, named after Johann Sutter, an Americanized Swiss, provided protection to the many wagon trains that pulled in almost daily. It was located on the American fork of the Sacramento River.

Along with the fort, Sutter had built a tannery, mill, and, most important of all to the thirsty travellers, a distillery. Sutter did all in his power to aid the immigrants and his influence was so strong in the Sacramento Valley that the Mexicans who controlled California were powerless to act against him.

James Marshall went to work for John Sutter as a wagon and furniture maker.

But Marshall, like the hundreds of other people who flooded into Sutter's fort, hoped to find his own pot of gold among the streams of the Sacramento Valley.

It was almost a trick of fate that brought Marshall his success.

On January 24, 1848, while exploring the mountains, he spotted an object reflecting the sun in the bottom of a mine. He went to investigate and found a large gold nugget, the first one to be discovered.

While he tried to keep his find secret, it wasn't too long until news reached Sutter's Fort and Marshall's dreams of riches came to a shattering end.

He was hounded by treasure seekers and he fled to the safety of the mountains. When he returned months later from his retreat, what he found left him shattered. The mill where he first found the nugget had been destroyed by looters.

Marshall returned home to New Jersey, licking his wounds, his dreams of gold lying dead beneath the dry riverbed in California.

Back in Lambertville, he did a little gold prospecting but found nothing.

But the lure of gold sent Marshall back to California in the hope of recouping his losses.

Tragically he found nothing, despite all his efforts. But in recognition of being the first person to discover gold, the state of California gave him a pension.

The proud James Marshall, the Jerseyman who touched off the California Gold Rush, died a solitary man, his fortune counted only in hundreds of dollars.

The New Jersey Lifesaving Service

SHIPS AND THE sea have always played a major part in the history of New Jersey. With our state strategically located between the great ports of New York and Philadelphia, the sea trade has been instrumental in the growth of the region.

But with the increase in shipping, numerous disasters have taken place off the Jersey coast with great loss of both men and ships.

Between April, 1839 and July, 1848, 68 ships, 88 brigs and 140 schooners were wrecked from the South Jersey shore all the way to Long Island Sound.

To make matters worse, nature is not kind to the South

Jersey shore. The shore is buffeted by strong northeasterly winds blowing in off the Atlantic. A short way out to sea runs a sand bar 300-800 yards in length and 2 feet below the water.

These dangerous conditions unknown to many a ship's captain meant the end of his ship.

In order to combat the ever increasing ship disasters, the early settlers of New Jersey set up a lifesaving network along the Jersey shore.

One of the earliest lifesaving stations was built at Long Beach Island at Harvey Ceders in 1848. Other stations were soon constructed a short distance away at Beach Haven, Ship Bottom and Barnegat City.

These early stations were crude in design and were understaffed. They were small, usually 20 by 40 feet long, shaped like barns and painted brick red.

For their size, these stations carried a large arsenal of equipment. Each house had surfboats which were dragged into the sea to rescue stranded ships. Each crew carried 360 fathoms of rope, a 600 yard rocket line that was shot out to grasp a sinking ship and extra food to feed the survivors.

If there were one man who was responsible above all for the growth of the service, the honor goes to William Newell.

As a young man, William Newell witnessed an event that would stay with him for the rest of his life. Watching from the shore one stormy day, he saw a large ship founder and sink in the Atlantic off Long Beach Island on August 13, 1839. Thinking how helpless he felt in not being able to save the crew, he decided to try to spare others from the same fate.

Newell came from Ocean County, a doctor who practiced in Manahawkin until 1844 when he moved to Trenton.

In 1846, Newell was elected to Congress, representing the Second District, which ran from Sandy Hook to Little Egg Harbor. Now that he was in a position to influence events, he decided to introduce a bill in Congress that would aid ships in distress.

In his first speech to the House in 1848, William Newell called for a bill to establish a U.S. Lifesaving Service. No such organization existed and Newell told his colleagues that it was imperative that one be put in operation. But to his regret not one member of the New Jersey delegation supported him. He tried every legislative trick he could think of, even attaching amendments to various bills, but they all failed.

But Newell finally succeeded in attaching his amendment to the Senate Lighthouse Bill in the House. The bill provided for surfboats, carronades and other safety equipment to be established along the shore to aid in preventing shipwrecks. A total of $10,000 was voted to fund the new organization

Newell now began to tinker with lifesaving equipment and he invented a lifeline gun in which a motorball carried a line from shore to a ship in trouble and towed it to safety.

As the Lifesaving Service expanded, stations were set up from Little Egg Harbor to Cape May and north toward Long Island, New York.

By 1870, the service employed a six man crew to run each station along the shore. But these men worked only part time only from December through February or the "winter season," the time of the roughest weather at sea.

Soon the U.S. Army began to operate its storm signal system that was connected to each station with telegraph lines running directly to the buildings.

The work was hard and poorly paid. A worker received, on average, $40.00 a month and by 1900 the salary had risen to $65.00.

By the turn of the century, the Lifesaving Service had expanded to a full time job with crews manning the stations 12 months a year.

As written in the Newell Bill, the duties of the Lifesaving Service included the protection of life and property along the shore. The Revenue Cutter Service protected the coast and enforced the Federal Customs Laws.

The services were combined on January 28, 1915, by an act of Congress, to form the modern day U.S. Coast Guard.

In 1861, William Newell was appointed superintendent of the Lifesaving Service by President Lincoln.

After leaving Congress, William Newell became President Lincoln's personal physician in the White House.

In 1865, he returned to New Jersey and was elected governor.

Later, in 1865, President Hayes appointed Newell governor of the Washington Territory. Thus, William Newell became governor of two different states.

During his lifetime, William Newell was able to fulfill his dream of making the Jersey shore a little safer for all those who ply its waters.

New Jersey Between Jackson and Lincoln

THE YEARS 1844–1861 saw much growth in the size of the United States as the country expanded across the continent, acquiring Texas, New Mexico, Arizona and California. It was also a turbulent period in national politics as old parties faded away and new alliances were formed. The issue of slavery burned deep in the fabric of society and flare up into the bloody Civil War.

The people of New Jersey were caught up in their own growth and their politics reflected the national mood.

Between 1844 and 1861, the population of the state grew from 373,000 to 489,000. New immigrants came here and the cities began to take on the characters that would later make them successful in commerce.

Despite Democrat James Polk's election to the Presidency in 1844, the new Whig Party came to power in New Jersey. The voters cast their ballots for Polk's opponents, Henry Clay and Theodore Frelinghuysen. Charles Stratton, a Whig, was elected governor and the Whigs controlled both houses of the state legislature. The political philosophy of the Whigs reflected the changing times in the nation.

The city of Newark was also the prime market for the Southern states.

But the anti-slavery feeling ran so high that the New Jersey legislature passed a resolution in 1847 asking the members of the New Jersey delegation to the U.S. Congress to oppose slavery in any new territories that would be taken from Mexico, thus supporting the Wilmont Proviso.

As the decade of the 1850's dawned, a new political realignment began in New Jersey. The last hurrah of the Whigs took place in the election of 1848 when they carried the state in the presidential election for Zachary Taylor. But for the next ten years the Democrats returned to power, taking control of the state Senate and the General Assembly. The rise of the Democrats all but destroyed the power of the Whigs in New Jersey as well as throughout the nation.

The Republicans were opposed to slavery and, in New Jersey, with its strong anti-slavery feeling, the party gained rapidly.

On June 17, 1856, the Republican convention was held in Philadelphia to name its candidates for national office. It nominated the very popular John C. Fremont, the explorer who mapped the West and help conquer California. Fremont chose as his running mate William Dayton of New Jersey.

William Dayton was born in Basking Ridge and was a graduate of Princeton. He served as a lawyer and later as an associate judge of the New Jersey Supreme Court. Before he ran with Fremont as vice president, Dayton had previously been a U.S. Senator. Although the Fremont-Dayton ticket lost to James Buchanan, William Dayton had made his mark on the national scene and would later play a pivotal role in choosing the next president of the United States.

When the Republicans next met in 1860 to choose a candidate for president, the party faced a bitter battle for the nomination.

At the Chicago convention, the two leading candidates were Abraham Lincoln and William Seward. Seward had angered the South by his so called "irrepressible conflict" speech in which he denounced slavery as unjust and cruel.

On the other hand, Abraham Lincoln was viewed as an honorable man with few political enemies.

But Lincoln knew he had to negotiate with the power brokers and William Dayton was one of them. Dayton, knowing the close political relationship Seward had with Thurlow Weed, a powerful Whig figure in New York whose reputation was somewhat questionable, believed that even if nominated, Seward couldn't carry the Northeast, including New Jersey.

The Republicans believed in the protection of U.S. manufacturers and opposed the extension of slavery in any territory newly acquired by the United States.

As the United States moved toward war with Mexico, the people of New Jersey reacted positively. The sentiment of the population was in favor of the conflict and saw that it satisfied the need toward westward expansion. They applauded President Polk's so-called policy of Manifest Destiny and yet realized the dangers of this policy.

Those dangers lay right around the corner and it was a neighboring congressman from Pennsylvania that would light the spark that would eventually lead to Civil War.

Representative David Wilmont, a Democrat, introduced into the House of Representatives his famous "Wilmont Proviso" which caused an immediate uproar in the country. The proviso said that no slavery shall exist in any lands taken from Mexico by the United States in any treaty negotiations. The bill died in the Senate but was supported by many Northern Democrats.

As the people of New Jersey viewed the conflict set up by David Wilmont, they knew they would have a difficult decision to face. New Jersey had close business ties to the South, especially with the border states of Delaware and Maryland.

In order to stop Seward, Dayton threw his votes to Lincoln and Lincoln was nominated.

When Lincoln became President, William Dayton was named the Ambassador to France.

As the decade ended, new Jersey and the nation were on the brink of the Civil War.

Abe Lincoln in New Jersey

MANY IMPORTANT HISTORICAL figures came to New Jersey during the formative years of the United States. Those that stayed left their mark not only on the state but made a significant contribution to the country as well.

But one man who was later to be one of the most admired men in American history stayed only a little while, but his return to public life was a boon to us all.

Abraham Lincoln was elected to the House of Representatives for only one term, serving the people of Illinois from 1847 to 49. At this time the future president lived a spartan existence, desperately trying to support his ever-growing family.

Lincoln worked as an attorney, picking up the occasional case to keep the debt collector at arm's length.

As a congressman, Lincoln was just one of the many unknown men who came and went on Capitol Hill, men who would never be remembered except by their own constituents. His only claim to fame in Congress was his introduction of a bill to free the slaves in the District of Columbia. His bill died and was never reported out of committee. Frustrated, Lincoln decided not to seek reelection and returned home to practice law.

But he still had important contacts in Washington and he pulled as many strings as possible to find work.

He approached President Zachary Taylor for the job of commissioner of the General Land Office, which paid a salary of $3,000 per year.

President Taylor told Lincoln that he'd think over his request and would get back to him as soon as a decision was made.

It was at this point that Abe and Mary Todd Lincoln met some important people from New Jersey who took an instant liking to the young couple.

His benefactors were General and Mrs. Irick and Issac Field of Cape May.

Issac Field was an iron manufacturer whose family settled in Burlington County before 1700. The Field family intermarried with the famous Stockton clan of Princeton.

As the Fields got to know the Lincolns, they asked them to spend the summer with them at Cape May. The Lincolns quickly agreed and they all journeyed to the elegant mansion house in Cape May, overlooking the Atlantic.

This was a leisurely time for the Lincolns, a period of relaxation and reading.

Their new friends took the Lincolns around Cape May, past the large mansions and over the cobblestone streets that contained the sweet smell of the ocean, only a stone's throw away. They swam in the warm sea and collected shells along the pristine shore.

From this vantage point, the trials and tribulations of Washington, D.C. were thousands of miles away.

But one day in late summer a note arrived telling Lincoln that President Taylor had given the job of commissioner of the Land office to someone else.

Disappointed, the Lincolns said goodbye to their gracious hosts and returned home to Springfield and Lincoln's law practice, uncertain of what the future would hold.

The First New Jersey Cavalry

AT THE OUTBREAK of the Civil War in 1861, President Lincoln called on all the Union states to send volunteers to defend the country.

New Jersey answered the call to arms and, twenty-four hours after the Confederates bombarded Fort Sumter, Governor Olden dispatched 4 regiments from the State Militia to join the federal forces.

The First New Jersey Cavalry was approved on August 4, 1861 by the War Department in Washington. The regiment began as a private group not under the control of the state. The first regiment was called "Halsted's Horse," named after William Halsted, a prominent lawyer in New Jersey.

The First Jersey Cavalry left its headquarters at Trenton for Washington, D.C. Because the war was intensifying, the regiment was transferred to state authority on February 19, 1862. When the cavalry was under national control, it absorbed Captain Cornelius Van Riper's troops of the Third New York Cavalry, making one unit.

As the Civil War began to involve more federal troops, the First Jersey saw action in various battles around the country.

They served as part of the Army of the Potomac, in the Military District of Washington, the Department of Rappahannock, the Army of Virginia and as defenders of the city of Washington, D.C.

Many colorful and fine officers led the First Jersey Cavalry. Among them were Generals Samuel Heintzelman, James Wadsworth, who had worked previously with Senator Daniel Webster, George Bayard, who carried into battle the scar from a Kiowa Indian arrowhead wound in his cheek, and Philip Sheridan, one of the most famous officers of the Civil War.

The Civil War attracted many foreign military officers who sailed to the United States to help the Union.

In October, 1861, a Prussian-trained officer, Lieutenant-Colonel Joseph Karge, took command of the First Jersey. Karge had his hands full in molding the unit into a fighting force because the men lacked experience in teamwork, although they were tough fighters.

Another foreign officer to lead the Cavalry was Sir Percy Wyndham, who, in February, 1862, replaced William Halsted. Wyndham was an Englishman who had previously served in the French Revolution and in the French Navy, and also served with Garibaldi.

Sir Percy was well liked by his men. He was wounded in the leg in an attack on Brandy Station in 1863 and subsequently left the unit.

The fact that the First Jersey was led by so many foreign

officers wasn't missed by the press, who saw a good story in the making.

Among the papers was the *New Brunswick Times,* which criticized the Cavalry for having to rely on "foreigners" to lead them in battle.

Whether or not the criticism had an effect on the men is not known, but in September, 1861, an American officer, Hugh Janeway, took command. Janeway, at 21, was the youngest officer to lead the First Jersey.

At the Battle of Sulpher Springs in 1863, Janeway and the First Cavalry held off a rebel flank attack which otherwise would have crushed the nearby Union forces.

Tragically, Hugh Janeway, a full Colonel at 22, was wounded for the twelfth time in 1864 and died while fighting a battle near Petersburg, Virginia.

Five years after the Civil War ended and the unit was disbanded, Henry Payne, chaplain of the First Jersey Calvary, published a detailed chronicle of the unit. During the Civil War, the First Jersey Cavalry enrolled more than 3,300 men from all parts of the state.

Captain Paynes's account demonstrates that the First Jersey Cavalry started as a group of amateurs fighting men who but became some of the most skilled soldiers New Jersey ever sent into battle.

Philip Kearney, Civil War General

PHILIP KEARNEY OF Newark was one of the most outstanding military men to come out of New Jersey. He was a soldier, world traveler and an authentic hero of the Civil War.

Philip Kearney was born in Newark in June 1814, to a well-to-do family. His grandfather was John Watts, the successful owner of a financial empire in New York that combined shipping, mills, factories and banks.

In his early childhood, Kearney left Newark for New York, although Philip returned to New Jersey in later life.

He went to the best private schools of the day, including Ufford's Academy, the Round Hill School, Highland Acad-

emy at Cold Spring Harbor, New York, and then to West
Point. After being graduated from West Point, he was accepted into Columbia University Law School. After graduation, he clerked under Peter Jay, one of the most famous
judges in New York.

At the age of 22, Philip learned of the death of his grandfather John Watts, and who had left an inheritance of one
million dollars to him. Now wealthy beyond imagining, Philip
could do anything he wanted with his life.

He was a successful lawyer with a growing business in
New York and had social contacts who were more than
willing to help him in his career, but he chose military
service instead.

He entered the Army on March 8, 1837, as a second
lieutenant and was posted to the First U.S. Dragoons in the
West under the command of his uncle, Stephen Watts Kearney. Philip found the life at Fort Leavenworth to be exciting
and full of challenges. The West, with its vast range lands
and dry gulches, was as thrilling to him as the busy streets of
New York had been. For two years he led his men against the
Indian tribes that attacked the army posts and the ever-
growing number of wagon trains carrying settlers to the west.

In August 1838, he was appointed as an aide to Brigadier
General Henry Atkinson, the district commandant. In his free
time Philip met and was later married to a pretty girl by the
name of Diana Bullitt, who was the sister-in-law of General
Atkinson.

Wishing to advance his military career, Philip went to
France to study military tactics. He was posted to the Royal
School of Cavalry in Saumur, France where he learned how
to lead troops on horseback under various battlefield conditions.

Philip put his newfound knowledge to the test under
battlefield conditions in the most unlikely place. He was
asked by the French Foreign Legion, which was fighting in the
province of Algieria, to help in the capture of a renegade
sheik.

Kearney helped capture Sheik Abd-El-Kader, chasing him across the Arabian desert, and gained valuable experience. For his bravery he was given the French Legion of Honor, becoming the first U.S. citizen to be awarded this decoration.

After the Algerian adventure, he moved back to Paris where he and Diana resumed their lives. In Paris, Kearney played host to a large number of visiting American army officers, such as Robert E. Lee and Stonewall Jackson.

By 1844, the Kearneys had returned to the United States and Philip was again given command of the First Dragoons. But his assignment was controversial. Upon his return home he had a heated argument with General Winfield Scott, the Army Commander. It was only in deference to Kearney's family connections and his heroics in France that General Scott didn't take stronger action.

Kearney quickly took command of the Dragoons and molded them into a firstrate fighting force. He raised their morale and lowered the rate of court martials among them, which had previously been high.

By October 1845, Kearney had had enough of the Army and retired with Diana and their children to New York.

But when the United States declared war on Mexico later that year he quickly returned to service. The Mexican War led to Kearney's fame and a serious injury that would be with him for the rest of his life.

In 1847, Kearney's troops were given the job of escorting General Scott's men to the Mexican city of Verz Cruz. In August, General Scott took his 9,000 men to the Mexican city of Churubusca, an important junction that straddled two roads that led to Mexico City.

In the ensuing battle, Kearney was shot in the arm and the limb had to be amputated.

Dejected, he returned home to New York and his family. But his long absences from Diana took their toll and in August, 1849, she left him. They were later divorced.

Philip now worked in New York as head of the Army recruiting station at Pearl Street in lower Manhattan.

But, longing for action, he got a field command again and headed west in July 1851 to fight the Rouge River Indians.

But his old enemy, General Scott, reared his head once more. General Scott, still smarting over Kearney's stinging attack from years before, refused to promote him and Kearney left the Army.

In the years after he left the Army and before the outbreak of the Civil War, Kearney traveled around the world and married Agnes Maxwell, whom he met in Paris.

When the Civil War broke out, he volunteered but was rejected by both the U.S. Army and the New York Militia.

But he found a welcome in New Jersey and was appointed a brigadier in the First New Jersey Brigade.

He served gallantly in various battles against the South, fighting at Manassas, in the Pennsylvania campaign and at the Battle of Bull Run.

At the Battle of Chantilly, Kearney decided to be his own scout and he rode ahead of the troops surveying the terrain.

He was shot and killed on September 1, 1862 near the town of Chantilly by a Confederate sniper.

To show his respect for an old friend, albeit one on the opposing side, General Robert E. Lee sent Kearney's body back to the Union lines under a flag of truce.

His funeral procession was one of the largest in the history of Newark. Shops closed for the day and thousands of people lined the streets to pay their last respects to their native son.

General Judson Kilpatrick,
New Jersey's Fighting Soldier

ONE OF THE most famous and controversial Civil War
Generals was Judson Kilpatrick of Sussex County.

Judson Kilpatrick loved military life. He left his home in
the woods of rugged Sussex County and joined the Army.

He received his formal schooling at the U.S. Military
Academy at West Point, entering the prestigious school at the
age of 18.

At West Point he learned the art of military tactics, which
was to play an important part in his later battlefield experiences.

Judson Kilpatrick's time in the sun began with the outbreak of the Civil War in 1861.

When the Confederates fired their first shot at Fort Sumter, South Carolina, President Lincoln called up the officers from West Point, including Judson Kilpatrick.

His first combat action occurred at the Battle of Big Bethel, Virginia, in which he was wounded. Following the skirmish, Kilpatrick returned to his Sussex home to recuperate.

As he got stronger, Kilpatrick returned to the war and organized a new unit called the Harris Light Cavalry.

He was soon strong enough to return to active duty and was appointed to lead the Third Cavalry Division of the Army of the Potomac.

At this point in his military career, Judson Kilpatrick took part in one of the most dangerous and controversial actions of the Civil War.

Judson Kilpatrick was young when he took command of the 3rd Cavalry. He was a dynamic figure with long side-burns and sandy colored hair.

He rode his troops hard, but was a slack disciplinarian when it came to their conduct. He was an ardent advocate of the Union and opposed slavery. As his reputation grew, Kilpatrick was given the nickname of "Kill Cavalry."

He was an ambitious man who had his future planned. Once the war ended he hoped to run for governor of New Jersey and had also set his sights on the White House.

Kilpatrick was not only a superb military tactician but also adept at practicing politics.

He brought together members of Congress to his military headquarters at Brandy Station, not far from the front lines. It was at these social gatherings that the General made friends of the powerful men in the country and preached his own political cause.

At a critical point in the Civil War, President Lincoln issued a proclamation extending amnesty to any Southerner who would return his political allegiance to the Union. He wanted this message to be distributed in the South. The

President also wanted to free the thousands of Union soldiers held prisoner in Richmond, the capital of the Confederacy.

As word of President Lincoln's plans filtered down the ranks, Kilpatrick saw the vehicle that would make him famous.

He let it be known that he wanted to lead the expedition to Richmond and volunteered not only his services but formulated a plan as well.

His plan was bold and it caused a lot of controversy among his fellow officers.

He wanted to lead a team of cavalry into Richmond, past General Lee's defenses, before the Army of Northern Virginia could send reinforcements.

While he was in Richmond, he'd free the prisoners held in Confederate jails and distribute President Lincoln's amnesty proclamation. Bypassing the chain of command, he went to see the President and the Secretary of War Edwin Stanton.

At the White House, Kilpatrick outlined his plan which was accepted by the two top men in the government.

He was given command of 4,000 men and told to implement the plan as soon as possible.

As his plan took shape, Army intelligence reported to him that Richmond was lightly defended in the winter, with new troops guarding the city.

General Kilpatrick's plan was as follows: General Gorden Meade would take a detachment of troops on a diversionary move toward the Alexandria Railroad while Kilpatrick would head towards Richmond. In this way, Kilpatrick hoped, the enemy would concentrate its fire on Meade while he raced for Richmond.

Another major participant was Colonel Ulrich Dahlgren, a 21 year old officer with a wooden leg.

Dahlgren's role was to take 500 men to strike the James River above Richmond while Kilpatrick crossed the city from the north. While Kilpatrick's forces took the brunt of the southern guns, Dahlgren's men would take the prison camp at Belle Isle and free the 15,000 prisoners held there.

On February 28, Kilpatrick left on his expedition. Along with Gordon Meade and Ulrich Dahlgren, other officers, including John Sedgewick of the VI Corps and Brigadier General George Armstrong Custer, took part in the operation.

Once on the move, Dahlgren's men rode toward the James River in a cold, driving rain that obscured their visibility.

Kilpatrick, by now near Richmond, sent flares into the rain-drenched sky looking for Dahlgren and his troops. But the storm obscured the flares and Dahlgren never saw them.

Kilpatrick nevertheless pushed on towards Richmond, battling enemy snipers along the way.

Kilpatrick arrived at the outskirts of Richmond and, as planned, opened up his cannon to alert Dahlgren, who was supposed to have released his prisoners by then.

But to Kilpatrick's evident surprise, the only cannon fire he heard was that from the enemy.

As the Confederates unleashed their deadly cannon attack, Kilpatrick ordered a hasty withdrawl.

Instead of the victory he sought, he now played a deadly game of guerrilla warfare against the heavily reinforced enemy.

Even though there was no sign of Dahlgren, Kilpatrick tried once again and sent his men up the Mechanicsville Pike but were driven back yet again.

While Kilpatrick was in retreat, the elusive Colonel Dahlgren divided his troops into two units. Some 300 men rode back to Kilpatrick while he took the rest towards Richmond.

No one is really sure what happened next but a sizeable part of Dahlgren's troops vanished. Colonel Dahlgren was later killed in a skirmish with the Virginia Cavalry.

Following his unsuccessful raid on Richmond, Kilpatrick went back into battle and rode with General Sherman to Atlanta and took part in raids on the Atlanta-Macon railroads.

After the war ended, Judson Kilpatrick returned to civilian life and was appointed U.S. minister to Chile.

The Strange Ordeal of
Captain Sawyer

WHEN THE CONFEDERATES fired the first shot
at Fort Sumter in 1861, starting the Civil War, the people of
New Jersey organized their own unit, the First New Jersey
Cavalry.

In 1863, members of the First Jersey Cavalry would touch
off a wartime scandal that would reach all the way to the
halls of the White House. At the center of the controversy
was Captain Henry Sawyer of Cape May.

In July, 1863, Captain Henry Sawyer, a member of the
First Jersey Cavalry, was wounded in the neck and thigh in
the Battle of Brandy Station. He was taken as a prisoner of

war to one of the most infamous jails in the South, Libby Prison in Richmond, Virginia.

Captain Sawyer was not alone in his misery at Libby Prison. With him were 74 other Union officers held in terrible conditions.

As Captain Sawyer looked out of his dark cell, he couldn't have imagined the train of events that were to come.

It was decided by the leaders of the Confederacy that two Union officers held in Libby Prison were to be executed in retaliation for the deaths of two rebel captains on spy charges by Union forces.

The two Southern soldiers were supposed to have been caught recruiting troops in Kentucky.

The two Union officers chosen by lot to be killed were Captain Sawyer and a companion, Captain John Finn.

While in Libby Prison, Captain Sawyer wrote passionate letters to his wife telling her of his plight. Mrs. Sawyer took her husband's letters to the press which promptly published them. Captain Sawyer, although known to only a few people in New Jersey, became an instant hero. In a short time, news of Captain Sawyer's plight reached the desk of President Lincoln.

As the publicity surrounding the case of Captain Sawyer spread, President Lincoln met with Mrs. Sawyer and a family friend, Captain Whildim, on the night of July 14, 1863. They also had a conversation with Secretary of War Stanton.

Lincoln, greatly outraged by the Confederate threats against both Union officers, sent a direct and firm personal letter to General Robert E. Lee, the commander of the Confederate forces.

In his letter, President Lincoln said that if the two officers were executed, the Union would hang Confederate officers being held in its jails.

What President Lincoln threatened to do was to put to death the highest ranking Confederate officers in Union hands.

The North selected two prisoners for possible retaliation:

General W.H.F. Lee, the son of the Confederate Provost General, and Captain Winder.

In the South, the *Richmond Examiner* asked Confederate President Jefferson Davis to order the deaths of Sawyer and Finn, thus aggravating an already explosive situation.

But soon public attention turned to the battles of the war and for months the fate of Captains Sawyer and Finn remained unchanged.

Feelings on both sides calmed down further as two members of the Sanitary Commission reported from Libby Prison and said that both Sawyer and Finn were being treated fairly.

Over the course of the next few months secret negotiations were begun concerning the Sawyer/Finn issue.

In March 1864, a prisoner swap was instituted by both sides. General Lee of the Confederacy was exchanged for Captain Sawyer and another Southerner, Captain R.H. Tyler, for John Flynn. On March 24, 1864, Sawyer and Finn were released and reached Washington, D.C., where they were united with their families.

After his ordeal, Captain Sawyer returned to the First New Jersey Cavalry as a Major.

After the war ended, he returned home to Cape May where he was elected to the City Council and went into the hotel business.

Stephen Crane

STEPHEN CRANE, ONE of the greatest 19th century writers, was a native of New Jersey.

Crane lived a short but exciting life, and left a mark on American literature that is still felt today.

Who was this gifted writer, a man who not only reported history but made it himself?

Stephen Crane was born in Newark in November 1871. The Crane family was well known in New Jersey and helped found the city of Montclair.

When Stephen was a child, the Cranes left New Jersey for a short time and lived in Port Jervis, New York, later returning to Asbury Park.

Young Stephen played baseball with his older brother, Townley, in the streets of Asbury Park, a stone's throw from the surging Atlantic. Baseball was only one of the hobbies that Stephen loved. Another was his fascination with the written word and that love affair nurtured at a young age would mark the rest of his life.

Stephen got his first taste of the newspaper business when he went to work for his brother Townley Crane. Townley had a news service between Philadelphia and Newark serving many of the newspapers in those cities.

Stephen, with his brother's guidance, wrote articles on South Jersey politics and local events.

He took his burgeoning affair with words with him to college, first at Lafayette, and, later, at Syracuse, where he worked as a stringer for the *New York Tribune*. After graduation Stephen moved to New York, the literary capital of America.

He found a run-down place on the Lower East Side of New York where he began the writing career that would take him to the pinnacle of his profession.

The Lower East Side of Manhattan was on the verge of dramatic change. Soon throngs of immigrants from Europe would pour into New York, where their forerunners were just beginning to set up shop. Stephen walked the streets, catching the smells of the ethnic cuisines that wafted from the restaurants. He watched the people and captured the life he saw in his notebook.

His first book was called *Maggie, A Girl of the Streets*. It was sent to many publishers but it was turned down as being too controversial. In the end, he had to publish the book himself. Disappointed but not about to surrender, he made a meager living by writing poetry.

As his name became known in the New York newspaper world, Crane got another job with the prestigious *New York Tribune*. Stephen's job with the paper did not last long, as he quickly became disgusted at the amount of corruption he saw there.

One incident he saw left an impression on him that would remain with him for a long time. Crane saw a city policeman arresting a girl as she got into a cab. She was charged with solicitation, but Crane saw nothing in her actions that warranted such a charge. He went to the police station and told what he had seen. Receiving no response, Crane wrote to the Police Commissioner, Theodore Roosevelt, informing him that he would bring charges against the arresting officer if the matter was not resolved.

But, unknown to Crane, he was fighting not only the Commissioner, but also the most powerful political organization in New York, Tammany Hall.

Crane's home was subsequently raided and opium was placed plainly in view.

When his case came to trial, the policeman was acquitted. Crane's trial for possession of opium sent the city into turmoil as people of all walks of life flocked to view the proceedings. In the end, Crane was also acquitted. Disgusted, Crane left New York for England.

During this time the literary side of Crane came to life. He wrote a series of ghost stories called *Ghosts on the Jersey Shore* in the *Sunday Press* for the November 11, 1884 issue. He also wrote *Tale of the Black Dog,* a series of ghostly stories concerning a pirate ship at Shark River.

His big break came when he completed *The Red Badge of Courage* in February, 1894 and sold it to a newspaper syndicate in England.

The book on the Civil War soon spread across the Atlantic to America and he finally found the recognition he longed for.

In 1896, Crane was shipwrecked off the Florida coast and wrote *The Open Boat,* based on his experiences. The boat he was on was loaded with guns and ammunition for the rebels fighting in Cuba.

He later went to Europe and covered the Turkish war for the *New York Journal*.

In later years Crane went to Cuba to cover the Spanish-American War. While in Cuba he got deathly sick and was forced to return to England.

Crane died at 30 from a tropical disease he contracted in Cuba and his body was taken back to New York on the ship *The Bremen*.

Even in death Stephen Crane became part of the history of his time. The *Bremen*, after discharging Crane's body, was sunk in the great harbor fire of 1900 in New York.

The Roeblings of Trenton

JOHN A. ROEBLING, a wire manufacturer and bridge builder from Trenton, stood on the Brooklyn side of the East River one cold day in February 1869 and stared intently at the frigid water separating Manhattan from Brooklyn. As he concentrated on the many ships that passed by, he began to think of a way to connect the two boroughs, something he had long dreamed of.

At that time, the only way to travel between the two boroughs was by ferry boat across the river. But traveling by ferry was a slow and sometimes dangerous process. In the winter, the ferry had to push their way through the ice that lay in the harbor and at times they got caught, leaving their cold passengers to walk across the ice or wait for a tug boat to free them.

John Roebling, an engineer who had successfully built bridges in other cities in the United States, thought of a new way to cross the river in New York: a suspension bridge that would be the largest in the world. He knew it was feasible. So he set to work.

In February of 1869, Roebling called together a number of qualified engineers to run a feasibility study on his plans for a bridge. During the first year the team met at least six times, painstakingly going over Roebling's plans. In the end they all agreed that a bridge could be built to span the two boroughs.

John Roebling came to the United States from Muhlhausen, Germany in 1849, at the age of 43. He first settled in Saxonburg, Pennsylvania, which was settled by his fellow Germans.

He studied engineering and soon began to build dams and locks between the Ohio river and the Great Lakes. Through hard work he became the principal assistant to the Chief Engineer of Pennsylvania and worked on various projects in the Alleghenies. In 1844 he built a wooden suspension aqueduct across the Allegheny River. He later built other suspension aqueducts over the Hudson and Delaware Canals, thus joining the coalfields of Pennsylvania to the Hudson.

Roebling then moved to Pittsburg where he built the Smithfield Street Bridge and set up his new home.

But the crowning achievement of his life was the bridge he constructed over the Niagara River that carried locomotives and railroad cars.

He now turned his attention to the biggest challenge yet, a bridge spanning the East River.

John Roebling chose his son Washington to be his chief aide. The young Roebling had studied engineering under his father's tutelage and was ready to take up the task.

Both father and son soon became familiar figures along the Brooklyn docks taking sightings and laying out the master plan for the bridge.

By this time Roebling had moved to Trenton where he developed a successful wire business and commuted between Jersey and Brooklyn.

But John Roebling never lived to see his dream come true. In a freak accident he caught his foot in a ferry slip and was crushed by a docking boat. He died soon after, leaving the work of building the bridge to his son, Washington.

In the summer of his death in 1869, Brooklyn was a separate city from New York. It had its own mayor, schools, police and politics. Its population was 400,000, less than half that of Manhattan. It was the third largest city in the United States, with a thriving port, even larger than that of its giant neighbor across the river.

Washington Roebling made instant friends with the leading opinion-makers in Brooklyn, including the mayor, William Kingsley, a contractor who paved Brooklyn's streets, Henry Murphy, a diplomat, Boss Hugh McLaughlin, and Roebling's most ardent fan, Thomas Kinsella, the editor of the *Brooklyn Eagle*.

Kinsella saw the building of the new bridge as the most important economic and political step the city could take. In numerous editorials he extolled the Roeblings and reported the progress of their work.

Politics played a large part in the bridge project, which Washington Roebling had to live with. The most important politician in New York with whom he had to deal was William Marcy Tweed, who saw in the bridge project not only prestige for New York but money to be made, mostly for himself. Tweed served on the Executive Committee of the Bridge Company and was instrumental in the creation of the company. He was able to take for his own use thousands of shares of bridge stock. If Roebling had any doubts about doing business with Tweed, and he did, he knew the political clout wielded by Tweed was all important and he could not object.

As work on the bridge progressed, Roebling chose William

Kingsley to be his chief engineer. Kingsley was a powerful Democratic leader in Brooklyn and a prominent contractor. He, along with the Roeblings, was one of the most influential people in the entire bridge scheme and saw it to the end.

The work began on the bridge in the fall of 1869. Washington Roebling brought together a young and brilliant staff whose average age was 31. He moved from Trenton to a house overlooking the bridge site in Brooklyn.

One of the many problems that confronted Roebling was the size of the bridge. Up to that time no engineer had ever tried to entrench an edifice as large as the bridge. Would the earth under the bridge hold such a weight? Would the fast moving current sweep the pillars into the river?

Roebling solved the problem by sinking a caisson deep into the ground where men would work. The caisson was made up of six large chambers with air locks for breathing and high powered lamps for light. Soon, 200 men would be able to work deep underground.

But shortly after the caisson was sunk the workers began to get sick. By June of 1872, when the Brooklyn tower lay 100 feet above the East River and the caisson itself was 51 feet deep, men began passing out, suffering from severe pain in their ears and other ailments. During the summer, Washington Roebling went down into the caisson and suffered a bad case of what people then called "caisson sickness," and we call the bends.

Later, when the cause of the problem was diagnosed, the workers would stop midway up to the surface to decompress.

Washington Roebling's attack of the bends left him partially paralyzed and he also lost some of his eyesight. But his mind remained fresh and, although he couldn't directly oversee the day to day work on the bridge, he kept abreast of its progress. From his Columbia Heights apartment, he saw the work going on, wrote thousands of pages of notes to his fellow engineers, directing their every turn.

For advice and strength, he turned to his wife Emily. Emily

was his ears and eyes, taking his dictation, carrying his messages and she learned as much about the building of the bridge as anyone. She exerted such a powerful influence over her husband that she began to be criticized in the papers and by Washington's colleagues. In 1873, the Roeblings went to Europe where it was hoped the clean air would improve his health. For six months they stayed in the crystal-clear alpine mountains but returned to Brooklyn without the cure they hoped to find.

Shortly before the completion of the bridge, the Board of Trustees of the Bridge Company asked for Washington's resignation.

He resigned reluctantly, knowing that his health was a major factor in their decision.

The grand opening of the Brooklyn Bridge came on May 24, 1883.

For Washington it was the crowning achievement of his life. The bridge was a part of him, as it was part of his wife and father. He had labored for 14 years on the bridge and was 46 years old upon its completion.

By opening day his health had improved and his eyesight had returned.

At the inauguration of the bridge, the Roeblings held open house in Brooklyn for the hundreds of dignitaries who paid their respects to the master of the bridge.

Under the new span that connected Manhattan and Brooklyn sailed the pride of the U.S. Navy, staging a noisy salute to Roebling's bridge.

At night, the new electric lights that had been installed were put on and the bridge was illuminated by a man-made sun.

The Brooklyn Bridge has survived presidents, political bosses, the wife of its architect, and will no doubt survive the test of time.

New Jersey's Marine Disaster of 1900

WHEN ONE THINKS of the great ship disasters, one turns to the well-known incidents of the sinkings of the Titanic and the Lusitania.

But one of the biggest marine catastrophes took place on the New Jersey waterfront at the turn of the nineteenth century. Before the fires were finally put out, four large transatlantic steamers had sunk and between 250 and 400 people had died.

1900 saw the rise of the city of Hoboken as one of the great ports on the Atlantic coast. The city had a population of 59,000, mostly German immigrants.

The Stevens family of Hoboken took the lead in building

the city and started the Hoboken Land and Improvement Company in 1804. This new agency was responsible for the filling in of the marshland and the development of a grid plan for the city. By 1863, with trade booming all along the East Coast, two large shipping companies decided to base their flagships along the Hudson River docks at Hoboken.

The two competitors were the North German Lloyd Line and the Hamburg American Line. They rented adjoining piers from the Stevens family.

The competition between the two seagoing lines was fierce and by 1900 they both were taking 250,000 people a year from Europe to the United States.

As June 30, 1900 dawned, all seemed peaceful on the Hudson docks. In the sky, birds hovered over the large ships looking for food and tugs took their cargos across the busy harbor.

Along the Stevens family docks the Hamburg America's *Phoenicia* and the *Kaiser Friedrich* were moored at the southernmost docks. At the northern pier rested the German Lloyd's *Saale, Bremen, Kaiser Wilhelm der Grosse* and the *Main*.

The North German's *Wilhelm,* the flagship of the line, was built secretly in 1899 at the personal order of Kaiser Wilhelm of Germany to compete with the British on the high seas. The *Kaiser Wilhelm* was the world's fastest passenger liner at the time. She held the transatlantic speed record, 21 knots in a 6 day crossing. This ship brought the North German Lloyd Line most of the Atlantic crossing passenger traffic.

In 1900, most ships spent up to ten days in port, refiring their boilers and making ready for the next voyage. At dock, these large ships proved to be tinderboxes ready to explode at any time.

On June 30, the Lloyd's piers held hundreds of bales of cotton, tobacco, and cottonseed oil, all highly flammable.

The wharves where the ships were docked were made of wood, 600 to 900 feet long, with sheds mounted over the river on wooden pilings. Many of these piers had recently been renovated and the old and new stood side by side.

At 3:55 P.M., the North German Line's watchman saw flames coming from stacked bales of cotton and sent the first alarm. There are different versions as to what exactly caused the fire and they are all plausible. It is believed that a stevedore working on the docks on pier three threw a match onto the cotton. Another possibility is that the inferno spread quickly due to the huge amounts of dust that accumulated in large cotton bins. The dust settled in the rafters of the buildings and spread below. By this one act, over ten million dollars worth of shipping went up in flames.

The fire soon spread over piers one, two, and three where cases of whiskey were stored. The highly volatile whiskey exploded, sending sheets of flame down the wooden docks. In twenty minutes the fire spread a quarter of a mile across the waterfront.

The *Saale* was the ship nearest to the fire. First Officer Schaffer cut the ship loose from pier two, which was now totally engulfed in flames. As the *Saale* left port her upper deck was ripped by fire. Miraculously, three tugboats guided her into the harbor.

A tugboat skipper watched in horror as the *Saale* drifted toward the Statue of Liberty. As he approached the ship he could see the faces of the trapped passengers in the portholes but was unable to rescue them. What the horrified skipper of the tug couldn't have known was that the *Saale* carried highly volatile kerosene that exploded when it met the rapidly spreading fire. The *Saale* finally ran aground in the mud.

The *Kaiser Wilhelm*'s skipper cut the ship loose and took her into the Hudson, but a barge of burning cottonseed still lashed to her bow sent pillars of heat into the *Kaiser*. The giant ship was seared and 200 feet of paint was burned away. In the end, the *Kaiser* survived with no loss of life among the 488 crew members.

The *Bremen* was the next to catch, the flames moving at a rapid rate along the blazing docks. The *Bremen* had carried the body of the writer Stephen Crane home for burial in New Jersey only a few days before.

The *Main,* the ship farthest from the fire, docked below Castle Point in the Hudson, didn't get clear of her dock and sank with the loss of 44 lives.

Sixteen lucky men of the *Main* survived by hiding in the ship's coal bunkers. They covered themselves with wet blankets to protect their bodies from the flames. Pursued by the fire, they jumped out of the open portholes and were rescued by passing tugs.

One brave act by the fireboat *New Yorker,* on the night of July 1, saved 16 passengers, who were heard pounding on the ship's hull and were rescued when firemen broke through burning cabins to reach them.

By 9:30 at night all the fires were out and over 200 people were taken to St. Mary's Hospital in Hoboken. When the hospitals were filled, the injured were taken to other nearby facilities, such as schools, bars and stores.

When the smoke cleared the devastation was discovered to be immense. It took eight days to put out all the remaining small fires and workers used dynamite to blow up the remaining Hoboken piers, unbearable owing to the stench of decomposing bodies.

But the devastation wasn't complete. Saved were the Hoboken Stores and the United States Bonded Warehouse.

While the shipping companies themselves couldn't have anticipated the fire, they did little to prevent it.

For example, all the ships that were docked had their portholes and doors open, allowing the flames to quickly spread.

In just one careless moment, the worst maritime disaster ever seen on the Hudson began, a disaster which left its mark on the banks of an old and mighty river, and the people who lived on her shores.

Woodrow Wilson, from Princeton to the Presidency

THE LIFE OF Thomas Woodrow Wilson spanned the years from the end of the Civil War to just after the First World War. It was those tumultuous years that molded the man from New Jersey who would become one of the most important figures in American history.

Woodrow Wilson was born on December 28, 1856 in Staunton, Virginia. His parents, Joseph, a Presbyterian Minister, and Jessie, who was born in England, schooled their son in the teachings of the church and a love of knowledge that would last the rest of his life.

His early years were spent in Georgia and North Carolina

where he got his formal education. In September, 1875, Woodrow Wilson went to college at Princeton, then a private school in the middle of some of the most beautiful country-side on the East Coast. Princeton reminded him of his Southern upbringing and he immediately became at home along tree-lined Nassau Street. He studied history and literature and became editor of the Princeton newspaper.

In 1879 he decided on the study of law and went to the University of Virginia. After graduation he set up practice and on a business trip to Georgia he met Ellen Axson. They dated and quickly fell in love and were married in June, 1885.

But he found little interest in law and decided to pursue further education in the areas of politics and history and enrolled at the Johns Hopkins University graduate school in Baltimore. During these years at Johns Hopkins, Wilson's interest in scholarship developed. He wrote a book, *Congressional Government,* which was hailed as one of the best-written books on the U.S. Constitution. This work made his reputation as a respected scholar.

Shortly after they were married, the Wilsons went to Bryn Mawr College, where he taught history.

But he wanted more out of life than teaching in a small Pennsylvania college and in 1902 he received the call that he had been seeking all these years. He was appointed President of Princeton. His inauguration as president was attended by some of the most important people of the day. Among those in attendance were ex-President of the United States Grover Cleveland, Mark Twain, J.P. Morgan and Booker T. Washington. President Wilson made extensive changes in the University, trying to make it one of the best schools in the country. He developed the so-called "Preceptorial System" of education where teachers were more responsive and friendly toward their students.

He also recruited professors from all parts of the country. These changes didn't go over well with the faculty, who saw in Wilson's reforms a threat to their long-standing ways of doing business.

Wilson served ten years as Princeton's chief executive, remaking the school into one of the best educational institutions in the United States.

But Wilson always had a deep interest in politics and at the urging of his powerful friends in New Jersey he decided to seek elective office. Among those who saw the young Princeton President as an attractive candidate were George Harvey, the editor of *Harper's Weekly* and the banker, J.P. Morgan. But if Wilson wanted to run for statewide office he would have to do business with the old line political bosses in the state, men whom he detested but at the same time knew he'd have to work with.

Besides being editor of *Harper's,* George Harvey was one of the leading members of the Democratic party in New Jersey. Harvey had countless meetings with James Smith, a former U.S. senator who effectively ran the party in the state. Wilson agreed to accept the nomination for governor of New Jersey, leaving the job of practical politics to Smith and Harvey.

In November 1910, Woodrow Wilson was elected governor of New Jersey by 50,000 votes. But if Smith thought he had a patsy in Trenton he was sadly mistaken. Wilson's first task was to rescind his support for James Smith's bid to serve another term in the U.S. Senate and he nominated someone else.

As governor, Wilson brought much needed reforms to the state government. He established primary elections for the statewide office, letting the people vote for candidates directly, rather than through the state legislature. Another reform was the Corrupt Practices Act that eventually took power out of the hands of the political bosses.

As the 1912 Presidential election loomed, the Democrats sought a candidate who could return them to office. In Woodrow Wilson, reform governor of New Jersey, they saw a potential winner. Wilson decided to make the run for the White House and was nominated on the forty-fifth ballot. In the general election he ran against President William Howard Taft, the Republican, and former President Theodore Roosevelt, who ran on the Bull Moose ticket.

Wilson was elected president, returning the Democratic party to the White House for the first time since 1892.

Wilson's presidency was called the "New Freedom," where he worked to curb the power of the large corporations and side with the ordinary people.

Wilson's first major headache was the fight over Protectionism. The Protectionists wanted to defend United States goods against foreign competition. The Free Traders were against protective tariffs and said that other nations would impose their own tariffs, thus hindering world trade. Wilson opposed high tariffs and introduced a bill to cut them in half. In its final version, those goods to be placed on the unprotected list involved such items as steel, shoes and farm machinery.

Another domestic action he took was to regulate the banking system by establishing a Federal Reserve System that gave the government the responsibility for monitoring the nation's money supply. The new Federal Reserve banks operated all over the country and ended the concentration of money in New York.

But it was in the area of foreign affairs that this scholarly president and man of peace was to make his deepest mark on history.

His first foreign crisis was with Mexico. In May 1911, President Diaz was overthrown by rebels by Victoriano Huerta.

On April 9, 1914, American sailors who were loading supplies at the Mexican port of Tampico were arrested for trespassing in a restricted area. In protest, Wilson sent troops to Vera Cruz and hostilities with Mexico began.

The next year, 1915, saw Wilson sending troops south of the border in yet anther fallout from the Mexican revolution.

Pancho Villa's gang fled north into the United States and, in January 1916, took over a train at Santa Ysabel and killed 18 Americans. Villa then crossed into New Mexico and Arizona and burned the town of Columbus, New Mexico with the loss of 17 Americans. The President sent General John J. Pershing with a force of 15,000 men and for a year they chased the elusive Villa across the American Southwest.

In 1914, personal tragedy struck as Wilson's wife died. He later remarried Edith Galt in December 1915.

When war broke out in 1914 among Germany, England, France and Russia, President Wilson pledged American neutrality. He deeply wanted to avoid a conflict with Germany but later events led him to change his mind.

As the war at sea intensified, and the Germans began their policy of unrestricted submarine warfare, American ships began to be sunk.

Wilson ordered the arming of the U.S. Merchant Fleet but the sinkings continued. In March 1915, the British ship *Lusitania* was sunk with 128 Americans on board.

In the election of 1916, the war in Europe dominated the campaign and Wilson, still pledging neutrality, but with his patience with Germany being severely tested, was reelected.

But an event close to home startled Wilson as much as any ship sinking.

In February 1917, the German Foreign Secretary Alfred Zimmerman sent a cable to the German Ambassador in Mexico saying that if war developed between the United States and Germany, he should ask Mexico to enter the conflict against the United States. In return, Germany would give back Texas, New Mexico and Arizona to Mexico. The release of the Zimmerman telegram sent a shudder up Wilson's spine.

In March, 1918, after Germany sank five American ships, the United States entered the war. American troops went to Europe and, along with their allies, defeated Germany and Austria.

But Wilson found the search for peace as difficult as any battlefield. In his Fourteen Points he called for open diplomacy between nations, freedom of the seas, removal of trade barriers, a reduction of armaments and pledged that the United States sought no permanent domination over Europe.

But his most controversial proposal was the creation of a League of Nations, a worldwide body that would work to prevent future war.

In January 1919, Wilson went to Paris to attend the peace conference, an unprecedented trip for a U.S. president to take. The League treaty was opposed by certain members of the Senate led by Senator Henry Cabot Lodge. Fearing the total loss of the treaty, Wilson had to compromise, causing the League to lose much of its influence. The Senate voted against American participation in the League of Nations, handing Wilson his greatest failure.

While campaigning for the treaty he suffered a stroke in Pueblo, Colorado and for the remainder of his term his wife sheltered him from the daily strain of the presidency.

Woodrow Wilson, president, scholar and man of peace, died on February 3, 1924.

The Morro Castle

SHE WAS ONE of the fastest passenger ships of the day, a ship ahead of her time. Along with her sister vessel, the *Orient,* the *Morro Castle* was known by the nickname of "Havana Ferryboat," as the routes of both ships took them between New York and Cuba, the ships carried mail and well-heeled passengers who could afford the luxuries the *Morro Castle* provided.

But the *Morro Castle* had secret side, one hidden from the passengers who frequented her decks, one that may have led to her disastrous end in the middle of a raging storm off the New Jersey coast.

What circumstances led to the *Morro Castle*'s tragic fate?

The *Morro Castle* was built at the start of the 1930's. World War I was over, the stock market crash behind, and Calvin Coolidge was in the White House. In New York, the port was bustling with ships loading and unloading their cargos at a fast clip. In contrast, the U.S. Merchant Marine had come upon hard times. It was quite close to bankruptcy.

Of the fleet of 1,000 ships that took men to Europe in World War I, only a few sturdy liners survived the passage of time.

Two of the ships of the line were the *Morro Castle* and the *Orient*. They were owned by the Ward Steamship Line, one of the biggest carriers of the day.

The *Morro Castle* was the best the Ward Line had to offer and in August 1930, the ship had achieved 21 knots in her trial runs and made her maiden voyage to Havana that same month.

In August 1934, the *Morro Castle* left her berth in New York for what would prove to be her last trip to Cuba.

After an uneventful crossing the *Morro Castle* arrived in Havana on September 4, 1934.

She was skippered by Captain Robert Wilmott, a 31 year veteran of the sea. Wilmott had served in various capacities for the Ward Line and had been on the deck of a cargo ship when the *Carpathia* struggled into New York harbor with the survivors of the Titanic.

For most of the trip to Cuba, Captain Wilmott stayed in his cabin, not mingling with the passengers, and ran the ship via his telephone.

Why such strange behavior for a man so well liked?

When the *Morro Castle* docked in Havana, mysterious events began to take place.

Ebban Abott, the *Morro Castle*'s Chief Engineer and a bitter foe of William Warms, the First Officer, met in private with the ship's doctor, De Witt Van Zile, in a fancy watering hole in Havana called Sloppy Joe's.

What they discussed is not known but the strange conduct of Captain Wilmott was surely on the agenda.

As the *Morro Castle* rocked gently in the harbor, Captain Wilmott had plenty of time to ponder recent events.

One of the reasons he stayed in seclusion was because he became sick from a meal prepared by the galley. He also thought of the attempted strike that threatened to delay the ship from leaving New York only a few weeks before. And then there was the mysterious fire aboard ship in the compartment that held high explosives.

Could there have been a connection between the three incidents?

Beyond the glitter of a first class passenger liner lay the darker side of the *Morro Castle*.

She had been designed for troop conversion at the cost of $3 million and, known only to Captain Wilmott and the Ward Line, carried arms to Cuba. These weapons were used by Cuban Dictator Gerado Machado to fight the growing Communist rebels who were threatening his government.

Captain Wilmott had one more thing to be concerned about. One person especially worried him.

George Rogers was the ship's chief radio operator and a man intensely disliked by the captain. Rogers had a hidden past, including suspected arson, which he concealed from his employers. He was an ex-con and was mentally unstable. When Rogers returned to the *Morro Castle* after his leave in Cuba, he had in his possession bottles of nitric acid and sulphuric acid.

On board ship, George Rogers told certain crew members that he was actually on a undercover mission for the Radiomarine Corporation to get information on how the ship was run. Rogers took his deputy, George Alagna, into his confidence and before long the young Alagna was repeating out loud every complaint Rogers had about conditions on board ship. Alagna even suggested that the crew stage a strike the next time the ship left New York. The instigator of this behavior was none other than George Rogers.

Shortly before the *Morro Castle* left Havana, Captain Wilmott received a call from Captain Oscar Hernandez, the chief of police in Havana. Chief Hernandez told Wilmott that his life and the survival of the ship were in danger from Communist agents.

As the *Morro Castle* sailed home, Captain Wilmott again took to his cabin, neither mingling with the passengers nor giving any explanation for his strange behavior.

When trouble began in one of the fire boilers, the chief engineer radioed Eban Abbot who tried to contact Captain Wilmott. Failing to get him, Abbot went to the Captain's cabin and to his surprise found First Officer William Warms in the captain's cabin.

Captain Wilmott was lying in the empty tub, half-naked and very dead.

William Warms, now acting Captain, was about to begin the toughest job in his career.

No sooner had the captain's body been discovered than a raging storm hit the ship like a steamroller. Winds and heavy rains pounded the boat from all sides and it was all First Officer Warms could do to keep the *Morro Castle* afloat.

And then it happened.

As the *Morro Castle* cleared the Delaware Capes, smoke was discovered in the writing room and in the library across the corridor. In no time the fire had destroyed the phone system and quickly spread across the ship.

By 3 A.M. an explosion occurred under the Lyle gun that fired a breeches buoy to another ship touching off 100 pounds of powder and propelling agent.

At 3:21 A.M. the ship stopped and the anchor was dropped at a depth of 72 feet.

At 3:23 A.M. an SOS went out and the abandon ship signal was given.

Two of the first ships to arrive were the *Andrea Luckenbach* and the *President Cleveland,* which quickly started rescuing passengers.

Another ship which heard the SOS was the *Monarch of Bermuda,* 20 miles away. But strangely, Captain Albert Francis never ordered the *Monarch* to turn around but continued on his way to New York. For whatever reason, he finally headed back toward the slowly dying *Morro Castle.*

BIBLIOGRAPHY

Books & Pamphlets

Beck, Charlton. *The Roads of Home*. New Brunswick: Rutgers University Press, 1956.

Boyd, George Adams. *Elias Boudinot: Patriot and Statesman*. Princeton: Princeton University Press, 1952.

Brydan, Norman. *The Passaic River, Past, Present, Future*. New Brunswick: Rutgers University Press, 1974.

Burton, Hal, *The Morro Castle*. New York: Viking Press, 1973.

Catton, Bruce. *The Army of the Potomac: A Stillness at Appomattox*. New York: Doubleday & Co., 1953.

Cross, Dorothy. *The Abbot Farm*. Vol. II of *The Archaeology of New Jersey*. Trenton: The Archaeological Society of New Jersey and The New Jersey State Museum, 1956.

Cunningham, John. *America's Main Road*. New York: Doubleday & Co., 1966.

———. *Capsules of New Jersey*. New Jersey: Manufacturers Insurance Co., 1974.

———. *The New Jersey Sampler: Historical Tales of New Jersey*. Upper Montclair, N.J.: The New Jersey Almanac, Inc., 1964.

Federal Writers Project. *Stories of New Jersey, Its Significant Places, People and Activities*. New York: M. Barrows & Co., 1938.

Field, John Perkins. *Halo Over Hoboken: The Memoirs of John Perkins Field as told to John Bailey*. New York: Exposition Press, 1955.

Flemming, Thomas. *New Jersey, a History*. New York: W.W. Norton, 1984.

Gallagher, Thomas. *Fire at Sea: The Story of the Morro Castle*. New York: Rinehart & Co., Inc., 1959.

Gerlach, Larry. *William Franklin: New Jersey's Last Royal Governor*. Trenton: New Jersey Historical Commission, 1975.

Hancock, Sarah Shephard. *The Story of Ship John and the Pirates that Roamed the Waters in Delaware Bay Long Ago*. (America): n.p., n.d.

Hoagland, Stewart. *New Jersey Profiles, Revolutionary Times*. Somerville, N.J: Somerset Press, 1973.

Ions, Edmund. *Woodrow Wilson: The Politics of Peace and War*. New York: Library of the 20th Century, Macdonald/American Heritage, 1972.

Kull, Irving, ed. *New Jersey, a History*. New York: The American Historical Society, 1930. Vol. I.

Lawrence, Frederick. *The Real Stephen Crane*. Newark: The Newark Public Library, 1980.

Lee, Francis. *New Jersey as a Colony and as a State*. New York: The Publishing Society of New Jersey, 1902.

Le Slie, Vernon. *The Tom Quick Legends*. Middletown, N.Y.: T.E. Henderson, 1977.

Lomask, Milton. *Aaron Burr: The Conspiracy and Year of Exile 1805–1836*. New York: Farrar, Strauss & Giroux, 1982.

McCormick, Richard. *Experiment in Independence: New Jersey in the Critical Period 1781–1789*. New Brunswick: Rutgers University Press, 1950.

McCullough, David. *The Great Bridge*. New York: Touchstone Press, 1972.

Myers, Starr William, ed. *The Story of New Jersey*. New York: Lewis Historical Publishing Co., 1945. Vol. I.

Nash, Charles Edgar. *The Lure of Long Beach*. Long Beach: The Long Beach Board of Trade, 1936.

Nicholson, Thomas. The Diary of Thomas Nicholson. Rutgers University Library.

Payne, Henry. *Ride to War: The History of the First New Jersey Cavalry*. New Brunswick: Rutgers University Press, 1981.

Perkins, Dexter and Glydon G. Van Dusen. *The United States of America, a History to 1876*. New York: The Macmillan Co., 1968.

Rose, Elbert. *Lincoln in New Jersey*. Bridgeton, N.J.: Yarnall, Biddle & Co., 1962.

Stellhorn, Paul and Michael Birkner. *The Governors of New Jersey 1664–1974: Biographical Essays*. Trenton: New Jersey Historical Commission, 1982.

Stockton, Frank. *Stories of New Jersey*. New Brunswick: Rutgers University Press, 1961.

Tales of New Jersey. New Jersey Bell Telephone, 1963.

Thomas, Gordon and Max Witts-Morgan. *The Strange Fate of the Morro Castle*. New York: Collins Publishers, 1973.

Tindall, George Brown. *America, a Narrative History*. New York: W.W. Norton, 1984. Vol. II.

Werstein, Irving. *Kearney the Magnificent: The Story of General Philip Kearney 1815–1862*. New York: The John Day Co., 1962.

Whisenhunt, Donald. *Elias Boudinot, New Jersey Revolutionary Experience*. Trenton: New Jersey Historical Commission, 1975.

Wilson, Harold. *The Story of the Jersey Shore*. Princeton: D. Van Nostrand & Co., 1964.

Periodicals

Cunningham, John. "Phil Kearney: Greater Than Legend." *Proceedings of the New Jersey Historical Society,* Vol. LXXIX, No. 3 (1961), pp. 149–162.

Gordon, Robert. "The Great Harbor Fire: The North German Lloyd Disaster of 1900." *Proceedings of the New Jersey Historical Society*. Vol. 100, Nos. 3–4 (1982), pp. 1–12.

Hoffman, Daniel G. "Stephen Crane's New Jersey Ghosts." *Proceedings of the New Jersey Historical Society*. Vol. LXXI, No. 4 (1953), pp. 239–253.

"Hundreds Die in Fire: Three Great Liners Wrecked; Costly Wharves Destroyed: North German Lloyd's Big Loss." *New York Herald Tribune,* 30 July 1900, Sec. 1, p. 1, col. 1.

Index
New Jersey History

Read All About It!

The History, Geography and Folklore of the Middle Atlantic States

Anyone interested in the people and places of New Jersey, Delaware, Pennsylvania and surrounding region can find a wealth of fascinating reading in the growing collection of books from the Middle Atlantic Press. And there's more . . . the mystique of Tall Ships, German-American heritage recipes, decoy art, historical architecture of Delaware and other regional favorites.

For Children and Adults

Read about the Amish, the Lenni Lenape, and the folk customs of the region's oldest settlements. From the countryside that inspired Andrew Wyeth to the treasure coast, from the land of the Jersey Devil to the Cheseapeake and Delaware Bays, Middle Atlantic books provide insights and history available nowhere else.

For Schools, Public Libraries and Your Own
Collection of Great Reading Materials

Now you can order directly from the publisher. Order your Middle Atlantic catalog today!

Write: Catalog
The Middle Atlantic Press, Inc.
848 Church Street
P.O. Box 945
Wilmington, Delaware 19899